Freedom

Is – (period.)

Release 2.0b

by Dr. Robert C. Worstell

Table of Contents

To all our many devoted and loyal fans:

We write and publish these stories <u>only</u> for you.

(Be sure to get your bonuses at the end of the book...)

- - - -

Look for addtional versions of this book in print, audio, and course formats. Ask your bookseller for the versions you want - see also the Related Books section at the end.

Release 2.0b

Introduction to Version 2.0

IT'S PERHAPS SURPRISING to me that it's been over a decade since I had much to say about achieving personal freedom.

Mostly because my life after this book first came out was mostly calm, usually peaceful.

Still the odd points of strife that made it "mostly" still reminded me I had more to study, learn, release. Daily.

I was publishing, running a working farm, testing out many things (among them, fiction writing for three contiguous years). And my work in discovering things continued. Among these was that the various materials of goal achievement not only got anyone whatever they wanted in life, but also built the core of what Western people seek out in inspirational materials.

To be sure, the breakdown of governments during the "Panic of 2020" and it's accompanying political strife was perhaps a necessary distraction and also a wake-up call that something in my life was still out of balance.

There's been no simply guidebook to gaining your own enlightenment. Levenson perhaps came closest with his breakthroughs. But there are also José Silva and several others in those post WWII times. One of those was Max Freedom Long, who revitalized the study of ancient Polynesian teachings with his "Huna" materials – and once these native studies and teachers were enabled to again spread their teachings after the late 70's, more material became available.

An old friend recommended me a book which started tying all I'd been studying together. And took it further. This book is "The Greatest Secret" by Rhonda Byrne. She took the time since her bestseller "The Secret" came out to continue her own research, which was compiling all these various enlightened teachers (Levenson among them) who had taken the next step beyond where most other self-help teachings have stopped their own journey.

What I update here is simply my own take on how to move from where you are – to where you haven't considered was possible. Because you were missing a simple datum. And because all the other most popular teachers in the our inspirational texts also missed. It's that step beyond.

For now, I'll leave you with this promise of going beyond regaining all the personal freedom most others around you gave up long ago – to having unlimited peace, joy, and abundance in your life.

It's all out there, waiting for you patiently. Just as it's always been.

And the point that philosopher made over a century ago can now be fulfilled: you cannot shovel out the dark, but you can turn on more light.

Prelude

OUR QUEST FOR PERSONAL Freedom is really illustrated well in this tale of the misadventures of a young Ivy League professor.

The story begins with an academic who was researching in his university's antiquities archive in the early 1900's and came across a misfiled piece of parchment. While it was in an ancient language, it was readable to this well-studied young man. It told of a repository of incredible knowledge which was found at the top of a remote mountain. In this place would be found all secrets revealed, all mysteries explained. The professor cross-referenced this data and found little except intriguing clues that the parchment was indeed authentic, and apparently hundreds of years old, and that the area it refers to is also known by other texts as a forbidden area with many dangers. No accurate maps of the area existed at that time. And legends he consulted backed this up with tales of a mysterious mountain where people would lose their mind in searching for knowledge and power. As well, that these secrets were stored in this one location for the good of humankind, to keep them safe and secure.

As the professor continued his research, this became a consuming passion with him. It started to invade his dreams at night - where he often found himself alone on a barren mountainside, ever climbing, despite torn clothes and scraped fingers, with a piercing, freezing cold wind that tried to pluck him off his tenuous perch down into the depths below.

Even his friends note his haggard look. His students start spreading stories about lectures where this young professor simply stopped in mid-sentence, looking off into the distance - transfixed by what he was thinking about.

The professor finally realized that something must be done. He arranged finances for this journey, calling in all his favors and confiding with key university donors about what he expected to find on this mountain top - the secrets to all knowledge, all powers of the universe explained.

Finally, he had just enough to cover a single person on this excursion, one his Dean called "foolhardy" even as he scrawled his approval for that professor's emergency sabbatical request.

Leaving notes for his friends and family, telling his landlady to not disturb his room while he was away, the professor hurriedly departed. His itinerary required him to take steamship, railways, and finally both mule- and llama-trains to the remote area where legend said the mysterious mountain sat. As he traveled, he asked the locals about the legend - did they believe it, where did they think it was. Most hadn't heard of it. Those that did just smiled and shook their head, telling him nothing more.

But as he traveled deeper inland, he found more and more people smiling and saying nothing. He knew he was getting closer and concluded these locals evidently were just keeping all these secrets to themselves. A few told him what he was looking for was incredibly dangerous - that the climb had often turned back those individuals who had tried. The mountain was treacherous, with screaming winds that tore climbers loose from their grip, and always shrouded in dark and forbidding clouds. They told of people who had never returned from the climb, leaving their belongings at the nearest inn, unclaimed. And others who returned forever haunted by what they had seen, strange looks etched into their faces...

Finally, the professor reached the remote valley which his research said lay just below the base of this mountain. Descending on foot down a zig-zag path cut into the hillside, he noticed that the valley was well organized into farms like a patchwork quilt as far as he could see. While the mountains surrounding the valley were cloaked in clouds, the valley itself was well-lit with plenty of sunshine for the growing crops.

There was one building for visitors, an inn of sorts, with rooms to let. In the main room were climbing gear hung on the walls - some ancient, some modern. One caught the professor's eye – it bore the inscription of a famous explorer who had disappeared in this area just a few years earlier. Yet it looked like it hadn't been used, just left for the innkeeper to care for against the owner's eventual return.

As his evening meal was brought, he asked his server about the legend. The old man's brow furrowed with worry and he silently looked deep into the professor's eyes - then the worry was replaced with laughter lines as his face lit up into a broad smile. But still, the old man wouldn't say anything about the legend. Instead, he merely asked, "You starting at first light?"

The professor nodded. The old server just chuckled and turned, hobbling back to the cook-room.

That night's sleep was restless, the old dreams returned. As he climbed the mountain in his dream, he made a careless error and grabbed a loose rock formation which crumbled in his hand. Just then the wind ripped fiercely across his back and buffeted him loose. He stumbled and then began falling—falling down into the foggy depths, flailing arms and legs finding no purchase.

The young professor awoke, sweating, as he "landed" in his soft bed at the inn. The first pale glimmers of light were starting to show and he heard the tinkling of bells as the herders arranged their goats for milking and feeding.

Dressing quickly, he almost inhaled his breakfast and went to thank his host, who was standing near the doorway. As his innkeeper opened the door, he stopped the professor. One hand on his visitor's shoulder, the old man raised his arm and pointed to the nearest end of the valley - where the professor could see a clear path that wound through and finally disappeared as it rose up into the low morning fog.

An easy walk, this fit academic wasn't even breathing hard as he reached the far valley end, and he saw this path become thinner and less defined as it took him up beyond the valley's edge and into the waiting clouds above. Looking up, he could only make out glimpses of the mountain side. He found himself at the edge of the treeline now, and only very shrubby, small plants held onto life in and amongst the rocks and boulders.

Suddenly, a touch on his elbow caused him to whirl. There stood a bent old man with a staff, his goats behind him. The man said nothing, but looked solemn. But then a slight, even wistful smile crossed his craggy face. He began to speak with a broken dialect, which the professor understood as composed from several ancient languages he'd only studied in his archives.

This goat-herder told him that the path ended here. He'd have to make his own way from this point. He pointed up the mountainside, a direction to take up to the top. The professor tried to peer through the clouds covering that direction, but when he turned back to ask for more directions, the old man was gone. The young professor was alone.

The next long hours were just as his dreams had forewarned. Sharp outcroppings tugged and ripped his clothes, while scraping his hands. The wind was gusting and severe, the clouds thick and cold - he often would lose sight of his own feet as he climbed on and on,up and up. But his feared nightmares didn't happen. He climbed precisely and relentlessly, careful to place each foot solidly, and ensuring each handhold was firm and secure.

Finally, he reached a point where there was no more "up". Casting about in all directions, he could not find another, higher grip. Moving carefully around the mist-shrouded rock, he could find no other hand or foot-hold which would lead to any higher level. Had he reached the top? Where was this monastery he thought to be here, or was some ancient book or roll of parchment buried somewhere near?

The wind increased precipitously. He quickly shrank back to secure his hold and footing, closing his eyes to concentrate on holding his place against the severe buffeting. It was then the light got brighter and the wind ceased.

He opened his squinted eyes slowly - to find himself holding on to a rock in the middle of a field, with flat pasture all around. It was a sunny day and goats were grazing contentedly about. Instead of mountain, there was only the broad field covered with native grasses and brush. A few feet away, he saw a goat-herder - who turned toward him at the same time.

Rising from the rock, the professor wiped his scraped hands on his shredded tunic and walked over to the goat-herder.

Surprisingly, it was the same face the professor had seen at the top edge of the valley. "Where am I, where's the mountain?" he shouted.

The goat-herder smiled and replied quietly to that young academic, "You are here, you made it."

Perplexed, the professor asked, "But I was climbing a mountain - where is it?"

The goat-herder smiled even more broadly and said simply, "There never was a mountain. You were here all the time.

"Congratulations - you've now arrived."

Forward

THE STORY IN THE PRECEDING pages illustrates the exact point which lead me finally to write this last book. As the professor discovered, Freedom Is – (period.)

Through all the books I've studied and lectures listened to - as well as my own research and tests down this line — it has become very clear to me that *we each already have all the Freedom, Happiness, and Peace we could ever want.* It's just sitting there waiting for us to recognize its presence in our nature. Just waiting for us to let our own light shine.

That's the secret people have been looking for all this time, the one which the self-help guru's will sell you unlimited books, CD's, video's, and personal consultation to help you find. But I think, like Dorothy with her slippers, you eventually find that you've had the solution all along. And also like Dorothy, you have to make the journey before you'll believe it's that simple.

This is the route to enlightenment which people have chased for so long, one which has lead some people around in circles, others to an early grave. Throughout the ages, enlightenment has been sought, and sometimes found. But these efforts often were hidden in musty archives. It's only been in this Internet Age that anyone can have access to vast amounts of data, both ancient and modern, literally at one's fingertips.

It has become not only easier, but absolutely vital that each person take what can be grasped and experienced from this "virtual buffet", and let the rest go. (Just as a thirsty person can't use the full output of a fire hose.) With all these resources so immediately available, any idea of having "the truth" dictated by any single person to anyone else shows up as pretense. And as you now have to choose for yourself, the truth within will to start shining out on its own.

The trick is this one, simple datum:

> *The limits you have, the only things holding you back, are those you have accepted. And these limits are all additive, not natural.*

All the Freedom, Happiness, and Peace you want is already found within you, so to speak. It isn't found by attending certain political rallies, or as a martyr for some cause. There is no government which can guarantee you any amount of freedom. No amount of money can buy it. No specific inherited DNA allows you to have more or less Freedom than the next fellow. And, likewise, no external person or thing can, of itself, actually limit your Freedom, even in the slightest.

The amount of Freedom, Happiness, and Peace you can have is dependent on yourself. You set your own limits to what you experience, every second of every day in your lifetime.

Check out any number of biographies and you will find these certain facts. The person's beliefs limit him more than any upbringing, family wealth - or lack of it. No particular race of people has had more enduring freedom than any other.

What is true of freedom is also true of financial abundance, prosperity, good health, loving relationships. Name a humankind condition of lack or want and you will find that the person themselves actually set their own limits to what they could personally be, do, or have.

However, the solutions to these conditions have been repetitively re-discovered and republished throughout history. Study all the self-help authors you can come across. Download and distill all their books into simple basics and you will find (at least in the true bestsellers) a common theme and common approaches to these problems.

And it's not just self-help. Take those distilled approaches and see if the myths and legends of history and pre-history don't abound with the same principles. Where there was any success, heroes and heroines were able to discard the accepted "conventional wisdom" and replaced it with their own unlimited ideas of success - which they then followed to make their mark in history.

Backtrack all the financial wizards and the multi-billionaires who travel or have traveled this earth. You'll find in each of them these same principles of unlimited wealth. Look up the people known as "healers" and you'll see they also subscribe to these principles, and their successes as healers are generally only with the treated individuals who also subscribe and put their faith in these ideas of unlimited health. Where you can, seek out people who get along with everyone they meet. Interview them and you'll find that they all agree that there isn't anyone they can't get along with - unlimited successful relationships.

WHAT ARE THESE PRINCIPLES - and how long does it take a person to find them?

Well, for most people, it can take an entire lifetime just to distill these. Others seem to be "lucky" and stumble onto them right off the bat.

For me, after a half-century of living on this planet, I've spent the bulk of it in searching and studying for just these principles. The last decade has been devoted to simplifying them down to a single core set, which anyone could apply. In this last year, I finally uncovered the missing perspective which should enable profound progress for anyone.

And so I sat down to write about it, because it's just too wonderful to keep to myself.

What's being laid before you isn't necessarily an easy task, while it is simple. It might involves a considerable amount of work on your part. Some may find that their results come easy, others may find that what they are trying to achieve seems nearly impossible. And no two people find they have to invest the same amount of time, or that they can even get similar results by applying the identical data. As the cliché goes "Results May Vary."

Several old sayings are applicable:

- The ancient Japanese would say: "There are many paths up the mountain."

- The ancient Polynesians tell: "No one school has all the teachers."

And, just so we don't take ourselves too seriously (though equally true in spirit):

- Alfred E. Newman would say: "What, me worry?"

These, together, tell of a story which is different for every single person on this planet. Just as we are all unique from each other (and even as identical twins have their own separate identities) so do we each have a unique path that we must find for ourselves to make this path up our own mountain to attain whatever Freedom, Happiness, and Peace we truly seek. Consider this book simply an effort to share various climbing tools.

So why, then, would I try to write a book outlining a common series of principles, only to tell you that it's different for everyone of us?

While it varies in the details, your path still aligns to certain natural laws which cannot be changed by any individual within this Universe we live in. Those people who have learned or stumbled across these natural laws and worked out how to apply them for their own existence on this planet - these have found out how to create any amount of anything they want to be, do, or have in their lives.

What I won't tell you here is that if you only apply a single law, like the Law of Attraction, or the Golden Rule, that either or both of these – or any other singular "law" - will make you rich, famous, successful, etc.

What you find as you climb your own mountain will be exactly what you want and need to find. And only you can do the climbing, and you are the one who must choose which branch, fork, or side trail to take as you climb. Not all will be fruitful. Some will be dead-ends, and you will have to backtrack. You're going to have to keep your eyes open for opportunities and be willing to learn and profit from the lessons coming your way. If you're like me, your "dead-ends" will teach you more than you can imagine.

But the only things which are keeping you from what you really want to be, do, or have - all that Freedom, Happiness, and Joy you seek - is only within yourself. Ideas and thought-processes and world-views which you've accepted over the years have been piled higher and deeper to get the exact result of where you sit right now.

What you see around you is what you've created. And if you want something better, you're going to have to re-create that world around you.

AS WE GO ALONG THROUGH this book, I'll try to keep it interesting, try to keep it short and useful.

In this book, I'm giving you the climbing tools you can use if you want to improve your life with, all drawn from all these famous authors and their stories which we'll cover as we go.

All you really see here is the best path I've been able to determine for myself as I make my way up my own mountain. But my path, I've found, depends on enabling you to find yours.

While I'm proud of the work represented here, and I believe that this book represents a rather unique approach, I don't write it out of any idea that I'm the first to walk this way, or that I'm even particularly very far along the path myself. I don't even write it with the idea that this book is any better than the books I mention and review here.

And while I consider that an important part of my life-path is sharing what I've found, the only one who can say this is truly useful, is you. Take none of this as gospel, just consider it as you can, and decide for yourself what you want to believe after you've tested it.

Each of us needs help from time to time as we make our way along. I've had plenty, and it's time to give back. Or, you can take it another way - "A person has to give before they can get." Meaning that where I or anyone else wants to improve their life, there has to be a lot of giving in order to make these things come about.

So this book is my gift to you. Pay it forward in advance yourself. See if it doesn't help you get to where you want to wind up - or maybe someplace even better...

I – Getting Started

An Introduction to Lester Levenson's Releasing Technique

BY THIS TIME, YOU'VE covered a great deal of materials. And I've given you more paths to choose from than you can count bees leaving to bring pollen back to their hive on a bright spring day.

We've already covered the fact that all the Freedom, Happiness, and Joy you could ever want is already within. And that these several authors above each laid out a path to make these your own in the Now, to let your own light shine.

I included all these classics I've been studying them for years, plus all the authors they mentioned. I even took up Bible studies I'd left in my youth in order to study engineering and computer texts. These few books I narrowed down to be my own chosen "path up the mountain." But like those college textbooks, there was always something missing for me (again, as I'll say over and over, disregard the man behind the curtain – don't accept anything I'm saying a gospel truth. Find out if it's true for you.)

While many had raved about Haanel's Master Key System, and Napoleon Hill had miles of testimonials – and Carnegie's continuing public speaking courses showed more people than ever how to regain their own self-esteem, and the Bible was showing more people than ever how to let the Holy Spirit back into their life – but for me, something was still missing.

Then a friend sent me a copy of the Levenson releasing technique one day. It intrigued me. I sent off for more CD's while I also ransacked the Internet for everything I could find by it's discoverer, Lester Levenson.

When I got through this material several times (these recordings are mercifully short, and there are only a handful of actual texts) – I found that I had an explanation for something which had changed my life, but I had never fully understood.

Years before I started on the studies which resulted in my "Go Thunk Yourself" series, I was still working for a major West Coast corporation as a personal counselor, but was taking a vacation to the family farm. Life in those days was tough and hard-scrabble. No real way to get ahead and keep what you made.

I never expected to find a complete change to my life on a sunny, Midwestern summer day.

It was something straight out of Thoreau – or his mentor, Emerson. While on a walk in the woods, accompanied only by the two family dogs, I was suddenly struck by a profoundly immense Peace. All thought dropped away. For an unmeasured time, I was struck by the quiet of the woods – even though the birds were chirping, and insects buzzing, while the leaves whispered in the breeze – my mind was absolutely still and I was completely calm and at peace with the world and universe.

This "accidental" result was so moving, so life-changing that I wasn't able to continue my long career in Los Angeles after that. All my life's work in counseling others hadn't prepared me one bit for what I had just experienced. So I quit that 20-year career and moved back to Missouri in order to study and understand what I had experienced that day in the woods.

The answers didn't come easy – I still had to make a living – so my research was very part-time. I even went to college and got a few degrees in order to study what the world considered a "well-rounded education" consisted of.

The original "Go Thunk Yourself" was an early step, as well as finding, editing, and republishing a few dozen self-help and philosophic classics as a method of studying their contents. I generally had it licked, all figured out. I had a road map taped out and ready to follow – but I still didn't have an answer for what I had experienced that day.

Until I was introduced to the Lester Levenson and his releasing techniques.

Here, Levenson described what was originally just a two-step process to quiet the mind – and reproduce in anyone the exact phenomenon I had experienced.

And such phenomenon isn't rare. I've seen it in several authors, and read in biographies and legends of that type of scene appearing and happening to people all through history – in every continent on this planet.

But no one had explained it before, or given tools to reproduce it that *anyone* could actually use – anyone at all. No special training, no special equipment, no riches had to be paid out in installments in order to learn how.

My path, for me at least, was now mapped out. I don't have to search any more. Everything has stared to line up and make sense. The most practical point is that everything has gotten much simpler – which is the way things go when you are on a right path (to my experience, anyway).

So the inspiration for the following collection of essays has been taken from those materials of Levenson's I've studied, as well as his students Hale Dwoskin and Larry Crane, plus others. I mention the specific books and recordings as I go. This series of essays which follow are just my effort to simplify Levenson for our age – and to apply what he said could be improved in his own teachings, so that you can get the Freedom, Happiness, and Joy for yourself, that have always been there, patiently waiting...

NOW, THIS NOTE: ORIGINALLY these essays were all posted individually on a blog. So while they are each true to their own point – and each was only included due to the points they cover – in various ways, the may cross and re-cross some of the same specifics.

Consider these as flowers on the same tree – however similar, no two are identical. Each contributes to the beauty of the whole.

Feel free to skip around as you want, although I've worked to organize them in related sections and produce a linear flow of thought you can follow as you see fit. Consider each section to be another branch of the same tree.

The point is, as all the authors before this point cover different aspects of the same principles, use these essays as well to develop your own system or philosophy that will help you find that "path up the mountain." Treat them as a buffet table of ideas and pick those which make the most sense (and are the most filling) for you personally.

And as the Irish say, "May your road rise up to meet you."

The Way: How to Begin – as Freedom Takes Over Your Life

WHEN SEARCHING FOR Freedom becomes more important to you than seeking the World and all it's "benefits", then this search tends to "take over" your life.

Of course, that's a good thing. Because all your own innate Freedom starts rushing to the surface of your consciousness and everything starts to align with it. Of course, as you go, you have to keep releasing the bliss that shows up.

These notes are coming straight from the heart, so please study them carefully. They may seem disjointed, or non-sequitur. But they are simply notes. I'm working to get these out and to you as fast as I can so that you get the main points which have to be told.

Let's have some basics here:

Negatives tend to disappear and get replaced by "less-positives". Because negatives don't exist – every time you say a don't, a can't, a won't – anything with a not in it, it's a lie. The universe only exists on positives and less-positives. The positive always exists, even in very low levels. The terms "negative" and "not" and others like that, are just placeholders. They tell you to consider the idea that there is so little of something that it might not be perceptible. Nothing, for all practical purposes. But there is always still something there.

It's like that analogy Haanel uses – you don't go into a dark room and start shoveling out the dark – you turn on a light. Dark isn't the opposite of light – it's a varying condition of the *lack* of light.

And so you can see the uselessness of a concept such as Hell or Damnation. Practically, there are interpretations of the Bible which say the worst place possible is just the worst you can imagine. (Some literal translations of the Gospels say that Hell was actually a garbage pit – which is probably the worse spot on earth for most of us.) Not that any Hell, Hades, or other Damnation actually exists – except in your mind. Practically, as Heaven is within you, so is Hell. Your choice. (Of course, this is just my idea – reject it if it doesn't forward truth for you.)

Now, a point of disclaimer:

These ideas are mostly directly inspired by Levenson's book, "Keys to the Ultimate Freedom", but also from his tapes as noted. Other sources are listed (and see the Resources section at the end). If something I say doesn't make sense, just reject it and move on. If you need it later, it will be there for your use. The reason for these two statements is simple – it's your own Freedom, Happiness, and Joy which are important, not mine or anyone else. For all you know, I've ceased to exist on this earth for a very long time by the time you read this. Dust doesn't care. History doesn't care. Death doesn't care. Legacies are built to serve those who haven't attained their own Freedom. So I'll be pointing out things – more as a tour guide than anything else. If someone said something important, I'll work to get it exactly and post it as a quote. If you want to look it up, then do so. (If I mention something that isn't on the Internet broadly, I'll reference that source so you can find it. But realize that it's not the messenger that is important, it's the message.)

The key point is that you find your own Freedom. No one can do it for you. You can't buy it in any store. No one can give it to you. You have to earn it. And this earning is by doing less and less and less. Hard work isn't part of it. Dedication is.

We'll be going down that road of having a "burning desire". Like tying a carrot (or the best treat you can imagine) to a long pole that you stick out in front of you - just out of reach. Of course, you keep moving forward to try to get that treat.

Freedom is like those sirens the sailors used to hear, but the sirens don't call you to sail into their rocks, they call you to quit spending your time sailing around chasing after treasures and instead start living in earnest.

As Freedom calls you, a lot of stuff is going to drop away as less important and less vital. Just let it go.

How to Get Everything You Really Want Out of Life – Easier Than You Thought...

THE TRICK IS THAT EVERYTHING you really want is already present...

Of course, my view on this - and how I write about it - has gone through several incarnations, and may still change. But I think I've finally gotten down to a basic line of application and theory which has undercut everything I've studied up to this point.

And I reserve the right to revise this without notice.

One of my first attempts at this came from a book I compiled, called "Mystic Marketing" – which does work where applied. Essentially, it has you hone your ability to concentrate on what you want and deliver this to the Universe to manifest.

If you're familiar with "The Secret", you'll recognize that many teachers recognize the first statement above is true. And to get anything else to show up around you, there just has to be a change in your considerations.

Of course, Levenson's releasing technique releasing technique is the prime way to accomplish changing your thoughts and calming the mind. Just acknowledge and accept what's there and let it go. Follow that by reviewing what it is that you want and release on both having to have it and not having it. As well as being separate from it, or having to be one with it.

Sure, that's all a mouthful. You could also just simply have it show up by just releasing all the time. Whatever "it" is.

But all the classics, Wallace Wattles, Charles Haanel, Napoleon Hill – even the real "old" authors such as Genevieve Behrend and her mentor Thomas Troward. All of these just point out that whatever you really want is already there – the Universe is in a constant state of delivering exactly what you've asked for. And old writings two and three centuries earlier – and even to points before written history – all of these say this same point. You already really possess anything you are looking for.

In fact, they all also say or support the fact that this Universe is only thought-created – and that all the life-mechanics we go through simply justify the thought. All the "scientific" studies are just ways to rationalize the miracles-as-usual which surround us. And all this scientific explanation machinery is foundering on quantum physics – where they found out that what you think predisposes the outcome of the experiment...

Our modern approach to this is to recognize that we perhaps haven't asked for exactly what we want, but have asked for something else. "The Secret" has several teachers saying to rephrase anything with a negative in it – which has long been known to NLP practitioners, but is actually an ancient datum: the mind doesn't recognize a negative. So when you say you don't want something in your life, it shows up in spades.

Don't = do not = do.

Don't want = do want.

Of course, our thoughts are often jumbled, because of the non-optimal mental habits we've been keeping. We've built up all these survival patterns of thinking to keep us secure and survive. And the Levenson releasing technique allows us to release ourselves from the effects of these perpetual thought circles which have been keeping us suppressed, un-free, unhappy, stressed-out, miserable.

And as you release more and more, the mind quiets. You aren't filling it with endless thinking any more. *Then* you can figure out what you *really* want out of life – and it begins to show up.

Until then, it's much like walking around the living room with the lights turned off. You know roughly where the furniture is, but not exactly – and your shins take a beating until you finally find the light switch.

Now, the ability to concentrate on what you want isn't actually something taught in our government schools. And to a great extent, we train ourselves out of this by watching TV and popular movies. We tend to deaden our mind, to turn control of it over to others. Which is why advertising found on these "boob tubes" are so inane and stupid. Psychologists Maslow and Cialdini worked this over quite well that our motivations are what we've been trained by our culture to accept.

This just brings my continuing advice to the fore – that you have to turn off the TV, radio, and put aside the national newspapers in order to start improving your life. (The Internet is OK, providing you use it in strict moderation.) All of the above just keep your mind excited and reinforce the bad mental habits you've been carrying around with you all this time.

You are going to have to release these mental habits before you can make any real progress in getting what you really want.

The Great Releasing Technique Experiment – Freedom with no cost

THIS IS NO EXPERIMENT, this is life at its fullest.

While this may seem adventurous to some, it is really every persons' adventure. Because if you are reading this, you are seeking peace, personal freedom, happiness, joy, prosperity – whatever you want to call it and in all its incarnations.

But I'm not here to simply parrot or explain Levenson, Dwoskin, Crane, Seretan, or anyone else. These are just my own approach to this particular subject of personal clearing – if you want to call it that.

The Rules:

1. Cut out all TV, radio, newspapers, magazines other than what you need to directly live your life. Sure, if we could create a cave with temperature control and sufficient food to live indefinitely, then you could cut everything out – all contact with the world for the period you are working at this. But realistically, no.

My own compromise is to live on a farm and by choice with little contact with people other than a very few close family and whoever I have to deal with to get the farm business done. My freelance is on the web, so I work at this. And try to keep from going down rabbit holes by staying focused with exact actions to do daily.

The idea is to calm the mind and not let disturbances set it off again.

2. Understand the various release techniques fully. Get the books, listen to as many tapes as you have to. Get all this homework done as you can. Keep these to hand as reference, but don't refer to them constantly. Get the basics down to simplicities that you can easily apply.

3. Release constantly. Everything that comes up – until nothing comes up at all. Find your intuitive Self – and work out how to release that as well. Release all bliss as well. You'll know when you're done. Release stuckness when you get stuck, if you do.

4. Take no examples of anyone else as standards or goals for yourself. Not Lester, not the Christ, not anyone. In fact, release all goals and all personal standards of behavior you had earlier set. Become completely hootless about anything and everything. Attain or acquire anything and everything you need by releasing.

5. When you run out of things to release, and the world is perfect all the time, answer: "What Am I?"

= = = =

That's the sum of it.

Doesn't mean you don't do anything, but it does mean you have to release constantly. Listening to TV or radio or any "news" just sets you back, as these are just distractions and arbitrarily give you more to release. You have to want your own freedom more than you want the world. It doesn't mean you can't have amusements – but these have their own costs in time. How fast you re-acquire your personal Freedom depend on how much time you devote to it.

What we are working at is to get as high as we can, as fast as we can – and that upper energy level will allow much faster releasing of broader concepts.

The key points are to get the world off your back until you are fully released. I'm not going to say you are going to become a Master –

that is between you and your Self. I don't say you are going to do or achieve anything. If you follow these steps at all, what you get out is what you put in.

- Get the world off your back,

- Know and understand the basics so you can apply them simply.

- Release constantly.

- And when you run out of things to release and the world is perfect all the time, answer the question: "What Am I?"

I'm not saying this is easy or hard to do. Your mileage may vary.

It is just the approach I'm taking.

How you Release – Simply, Easily, Effectively.

HERE'S A DISCLAIMER right off the bat: All I know is what I know. I haven't attended any seminars or special training in the Levenson releasing techniques. And I give great credit to Larry Crane, Hale Dwoskin, Stephen Seretan, and others for forwarding this subject and making more workable.

All I say here is what I've learned for myself.

My own training was being given a bootleg CD (a few, actually) and being impressed with this material. And then I went out on the Internet and found everything I could about Lester Levenson and his releasing technique. Through this, I found digital copies of out of print books, and other recordings of various quality.

But the truth of this as a very direct subject shone through.

There are two steps to the Levenson releasing technique:

1. Accept what is.

2. Let it go.

And it's no more complicated than that.

I and others occasionally have problems with letting something go, and in many cases it's just being stuck – so you let go of the stuckness.

Other than that, I don't see a big problem with anyone applying it to any and every area of their life. It does nothing but improve things.

Sure, I've been studying self-help books for years and was some 20+ years in a corporate self-help cult and before that had spent several years in Bible Study as well as being an agnostic and all sorts of other studies as well as a few post-graduate degrees. Now, well after 50-some years on this planet, the Levenson releasing technique comes my way and explains what I've been rejecting out of all these other studies – and actually made them all start working again.

But don't think I am going to tell you how this is any sort of abundance course, or how you can make be making money working from home, or use the law of attraction to create all sorts of prosperity, health, and incredibly loving relationships – because that's simply not where I'm at on this. Sure, releasing will help you with your business, with your love-life, with the abundance of wealth, with your quality of health – and help you get it all effortlessly – but: so what?

Once you get everything you want in your life, what then?

You see, what works for you is just that – it's what works for you. There are many paths up the mountain (as I often say) but no two are identical. Each and everyone of us have to make their own path, or find it. And that path isn't the same as the one the person on either side of you is using.

For me, Levenson's releasing technique is a key point to use in combination with other material in order to make my own progress toward personal Freedom – or Enlightenment (since Freedom is already within us – so is Enlightenment, actually...)

And this is why I also write about this stuff at length. Because I consider a few things to be vital truths - at least for me:

1. I am only here to help others.
2. Whatever I want to attain or have is best attained or acquired by helping others attain or get whatever it is that they want.

3. Finally, that the whole universe runs on these two statements above. Period.

Now you can and should disagree with me on any or all of the above. Because it's not true until it's true for you.

But I've had incredible gains after learning (teaching myself) the Levenson releasing technique. And so I recommend it to others – as many as will listen to what I have to say.

Since I hadn't ever told you how easy it is to release, I thought to tell you.

Cheers! – and Good Hunting!

The 7 Simple Steps to Releasing for Personal Development

(EXCERPTED AND EXTRACTED from the tape series "The Way" these notes describe a very direct manner of re-achieving your personal Freedom. And whether you're looking for life's abundance or how to get rich – it's all in these 7 simple steps of Levenson releasing technique...)

The steps:

1. Want Freedom more than you want the World.

2. Take all your joy from within by releasing.

3. Make the decision to go Free and then do it.

4. Go directly to the fear of dying and then release it.

5. Get everything from here on by direct releasing.

6. Be not the doer. Be the witness. Let go and let God.

7. Make your behavior that which a Master would do.

Once you decide to get moving on the path to total freedom, you will eventually make it out. The only reason these materials exist is to enable you to do it in a single lifetime, this one.

All the joy there is in life already exists within you. You just have to release all the limitations that you hold in place to keep this from showing up.

You set up the decision to go Free and just work at it. Don't resist anything, just push this right on up and you'll make it. Keep striving for this and you'll arrive. The more you concentrate on it, the faster it shows up.

All the other points – control, approval, security are all based on the fear of dying. Simply go to the central fear of dying – release it directly and completely – and the rest falls away. You have to quit trying to make the body survive – to exist through the body. (But it's suggested by several releasing technique counselors that you spend significant time releasing before you try this on your own – it has at times made people physically sick.)

There's nothing you want that can't be more easily and rapidly acquired (it will show up faster) if you just release on the fact of it's being there now. Look for anything that comes up when you accept the goal of that product or service being present right now in your life.

Don't effort at doing anything. Flow with the actions around you. You'll get intuitive insight on what actions you should be doing. Just be the witness to what is going on. You'll see the actions happening around you and you only just have to move with what you should do to achieve harmony in your own life and the world around you. Just let go of any effort and let the God in you do the doing that makes sense in the moment.

Act only in ways as a Master would. The more you just follow the Master presence which is already within you, the more will show up on the external "you" which everyone else then sees. You will then start intuitively to do the right actions, the necessary actions, the harmonious actions. And all things that you actually want in life will show up for you. What you want will change. What you want now isn't necessarily what you are going to wind up with – it will be a lot better, a lot bigger, far more of it than you want or think you want right now. Just get off the thinking and act only as a Master would. And let it show up around you.

———

WHETHER YOU USE HALE Dwoskin's techniques, or those of Larry Crane, or someone else – it doesn't matter. The point is that you find a method you can use on a continual basis. As you simply incorporate this into your daily mental habits, life becomes more direct and easier. Try it and see – don't just accept what I say. It won't be true until you've tested it for yourself.

Be the Author of Your Own Life Story. Truth and Responsibility

IT'S JUST TOO EASY to say life is an open book. Especially when you say that someone else wrote it. But practically, there is no way around the fact that you are the author of your own life's story – the plot is yours alone, as well as the actions of practically all the characters in it.

I've been known to remark - often - about how the Golden Rule works around you all the time, that it can't be avoided or negated – it just is. Regardless of whether you "believe in it" or not, regardless of your faith. It just is.

So that means, essentially, that regardless of your relationship with God, a great deal of what is around you right now is the result of your actions or inactions – if not all of them.

Now this takes you a bit beyond "The Secret" and what it said. Wallace Wattles (Science of Getting Rich) and others have made a great deal about your needing to be grateful for what you have in order to get more of anything you want. And that is all very true. But this concept above takes you a bit beyond that point.

It really takes you a step toward what Lester Levenson is talking about with his original releasing technique teachings. And this is where the common sense of "The Secret" meets the extreme metaphysics of Levenson.

The world around you, for all practical purposes (and within believable limits) is what you put there. If you've been critical toward others, you've gotten some criticism into your life in return. Where you've been caring and appreciative, you've seen some care and appreciation come into your life. Where you have open-handedly helped others achieve their own goals – you've received some unexpected help with whatever you have elected to achieve.

So with this we are seeing that the more responsible you are for the world around you, the more it turns closer to Heaven on earth. Because the Kingdom of Heaven is within you, as Jesus said. You just have to "let your light shine" so that it starts showing around you.

And that's where Levenson's release technique comes into play.

What is holding you back from simply being gracious with everyone around you and helping everyone in sight to be and do their best for the people who surround them? Our own thoughts are traitors, as Shakespeare said. That is exactly the problem we face – the prison for our soul is composed of those habitual thoughts we've kept to tell us how to react in various circumstances. Fear, anger, distrust, apathy, worry, anxiety – all these reactions are those we've put there and still hold in place.

Get rid of these and you can see and foster more good in people around you. And more and more of that goodness then comes into your own life. Because the Golden Rule is inexorable. Happens anyway. Like it or not.

Releasing just allows you to get over all those negative thoughts, releasing allows your own internal happiness and joy to show up more and more frequently. No effort.

The next time you feel like doing something to someone that you wouldn't like having happen to you – try this:

• Pause for a moment.

- Take a deep breath in through your nose and out through your mouth – slowly. Take several if you want.

- Then just accept that emotion which is coming in. Let it really show up in full – don't act on it, just let it be.

- Then see if you can simply let it go, release it.

- Now, go ahead and treat that person the way you'd like it.

Too often, it will easily ddrop away on just those few steps. (Hale Dwoskin, Stephen Seretan, and Larry Crane have more steps you can learn for free on how to do this over at their respective Levenson releasing technique sites.)

But as you keep this up, and constantly work to help others around you in just the way you'd like to have happen to you if you were in their situation – keep releasing all feelings you have coming into you which tell you not to act that way... Then the world around you starts to even out. And you'll see gratitude start swelling up in you for everything around you – because you are being responsible for that world and are appreciative of all that you helped bring into your life.

Try it and see for yourself.

II – What This Can Mean for You

The Less Important Live Among Us as The Greatest.

IT'S OBVIOUS THAT MASTERS walk this earth. And they don't particularly care a hoot about being "discovered" or "exposed". Because they really don't give a hoot about anything. They do their job easily, effortlessly, and live their life in comfort. Mostly unknown, they don't seek the spotlight necessarily – since that is a trade-off and can get in a person's way in living life.

The key thing is to let your own Freedom shine out from within. You don't hide a light under a basket, you let it shine.

The usual disclaimer: My ideas on this are just that – discount them immediately and make them your own or reject them.

There are some old phrases from the releasing technique which I'll repeat here. "Be not the Doer, Be the Witness." "Let go and Let the Universe."

You have to get your Self out of the way so you can let the Universe within you shine through. You already have all the answers to any problem or situation right within you. All you have to do is let it out. There is no effort in it. Just let go and let the Universe. Let the Universe what? Anything it damned well pleases.

That's the point. The You gets in the way. There is a way of intuitional living you can adopt (or not – your choice). What this does is connect you with a fountain-well of constant inspirational and motivational. All answers are there, all solutions are there. It's the

Universe just wanting to peek out behind that "solid" facade called Self.

The idea here is that it's much easier to go through life by letting the Universe guide you.

Your life could be that of a Master – calm, quiet, perfect in every way. Just try what is covered in this book for yourself.

Speed up and Get There Faster Without Moving at All.

THIS ISN'T SOME SORT of Alice in Wonderland scene where you have to run as fast as you can just to stay in the same place. (Although many of us may have had jobs which were like that at times.)

The Levenson phrase is "Don't release to get high. Go high to release."

As you reach higher levels by releasing, learning more and more to seek more freedom at every turn instead of more world, as you learn to quit doing and witness more – you reach a very high internal energy level where things will just start disappearing on their own.

The release technique is too simple. A lot of people have worked to make it reachable by others – since if it were complicated, everyone would know it. But when you grasp the basics, then it can and should become second nature.

The whole point is to get the habit of releasing to replace the bulk of the mental habits you have. If you have any emotion coming in, then release it. If you aren't at peace constantly, release whatever it is that you have your attention on (or are trying to keep from having your attention on.) You want to find your own internal peace (which actually comes from the Universe) and let it flow out from you into the world you live in. Anything that blocks this flow – just let it go.

You want to get to these high levels as fast as you can, since this will make that flow a torrent. Of course, any bliss that shows up, release that as well. It's not a state of ecstasy you want to achieve. It's a calm, almost serene and simple way of living where there is no rush, there is no excitement, everything is just fine, everything is just perfect.

And it's that way all the time.

So get releasing down to just a two-step process – you see something, then you let it go. Eventually, things just start cascading, as your internal flow just rolls things out of your system faster than you can even consider what it was that you had your attention on a few moments ago – but that's OK, it doesn't matter: the Universe is perfect.

Probably won't happen overnight. But you may wind up woken up in the night with some inspiration, something you have to do right now. As you let go and let the Universe, this will happen more and more. But it's always for the better – you're just going to get rid of some old "hold-me-back" habit and replace it with something better – or nothing at all.

Yes, this changes your life radically. As you are able to let these old things go, then your life will improve to that degree. The stuff you hold onto is holding you back. While we can't all necessarily just move off into remote caves or monasteries to live lives of quiet contemplation, most of us won't be called to do that. Just not the way this Universe operates – at this level, anyway.

The point is to be as responsible as you can for your own earlier mental habits and release these as fast as you can find them. Release being stuck if you find yourself stuck (just another mental habit). Release everything and get everything by releasing.

The World around you changes for the better – just to that exact degree you release.

The Unimportance of Importances

NOTHING IS REALLY IMPORTANT.

Sure, there are things you should do to keep living on this planet. But let the Universe show you what these are.

Take "your passion in life". Most people draw a blank when you ask them what they feel their purpose in life is – what they are here to accomplish in this lifetime. But that's usual. Most people have the bulk of the Universe walled off so it can't get out. Most people "work" at "jobs" to "make money" or "make a living."

And some people get paid to play baseball or some other sport for a living. They retire when they are in their 30's or 40's and manage real estate or golf all day, or some such. And the bulk of us these days have several careers.

I know of an organization that set about to find out the basic purpose of all their employees. They set up a huge program and put all their staff through it. But when the results started coming out, they found out that a small percentage of people were simply quitting their jobs as it wasn't what they really wanted to do with their lives. Of course that was a disruption. So management quickly came down with a correction that revised the program into "finding what their purpose for their job was". This apparently stopped the turnover. But it was trying to put a cork in the genie's bottle. (Frankly, they already had turnover all the time because people were frustrated from their denied purposes already. So their revision solved nothing in fact.)

I was one of those people who saw this and simply moved out of their way – into the Way which the Universe was going. Like was said earlier – you have to let your light shine. It's far easier and more comfortable than any corporate job working for someone else – unless that is exactly what you should be doing.

The Levenson releasing technique just helps you find and confirm your passion.

If you're happy, contented, and everything is going fine around you – then you are on the right path for you.

Because the world is perfect.

And this is why I don't mention earlier Masters here, or quote the legacy or writings of others. What good would it do? Someone pulling off a miracle just builds resistance in others so they can't follow as easily. Sure, if everyone were pulling off miracles every day, then it's common place. Like flying in an airplane, or driving along a road while you're sitting still inside a car. Or holding a piece of plastic to your ear and talking to someone on another continent. Miracles in the 1800's – not today.

Learn from the world around you, but more importantly, let the Universe already within you give you the lessons you need next. Let your light shine.

Here is one importance you can and should reject until you possibly can make it your own – testing it for yourself:

Whatever you want, give it away to someone else first in order to make it show up. That's one version of the Golden Rule. Treat others as you would want to be treated. Cheer someone else up in order to be happiest yourself. Help others be successful and your success is assured. If you don't have something, figure out how to help someone else get it – first.

Of course that flies in the face of any idea of competition. But competition is a lie, anyway, isn't it? "Level playing fields" are fantasies. No such thing. Winners simply out-create others. Sports are putting a bunch of talented people onto a arena where they are hampered by various rules and "now-your-supposed-to's" so they can excel to produce a very, very narrow range of accomplishments. The Universe isn't like that. Everyone excels in their own specialty. And there are just as many specialties as their are people.

So this of course comes in as: "many paths up the mountain". What is important for you isn't as important for the next guy.

Listen to the Universe within you – your own particular flavor. That's where your Freedom is going to shine from. And it's *your* Freedom, not the next guy's.

Get Everything You Want by Giving Everything Away

HERE'S SOME LEVENSON quotes:

> *"Let go of all your attachments and you'll be so light, it will be hard to stay on the ground."*

> *"Let go of all your desires and you reach the ultimate level of happiness. And when you put a thought out, it shows up."*

> *"Let go of all desires, all attachments and all these other things – and be free."*

> *"The more you let go of attachments, the happier you get – and the easier it is to get things."*

> *"We started out playing a game and wound up thinking happiness was outside of ourselves."*

Do you see how this works? Of course, the usual disclaimer: reject all of this unless and until you can make it your own, deciding and proving for yourself that it has use or applicability in your own life. That you can maybe get something out of it.

Now, the world is full of ego-traps. And the physical things you see around you are just the symbols of these. Money, houses, clothes, cars, planes, video games – all these things aren't real. Most of them would disappear in a fire or other catastrophe.

But a person who knows how to get them can replace them at any time.

A person who is dependent on them is devastated when they lose them – and even when they think of losing them. This person often doesn't have them and is just stuck in the desire for them. But even if they get what they want, they can't keep it.

Because they don't simply see them as symbols for other ideas. Money is a humankind thing. Doesn't exist naturally. You can't eat it, but you can use it to get others to give you food. Won't buy love, but you can get someone to have sex with you, or even marry and live with you for the rest of your life. Can't make you happy, but it can get stuff which will distract you from your unhappiness for a little while.

So the stuff around you isn't the real you. That real you is only what you find out it is. You have to start letting the Universe within you shine out.

Start the habit of releasing all the time – any feeling or thought about anything – just let it go. Use the release technique constantly. Then you can easily get anything and everything that you need or want. Precisely because you get off the artificial needs and invented wants.

Make releasing so regular in your life that you don't think about it, it's just second nature.

And quit efforting to get, or acquire, or achieve, or attain anything. Everything you really need/want will come to you if you just let the Universe within and around you bring it to you.

All this effort people put into getting stuff, that's just making it harder. That's a real game. Level playing field and all that nonsense. If you want to really win the game, quit playing it. Just let the game play itself. Be the witness up in the stands.

How to Make Your Own Luck

BEING "LUCKY" IS SOMETHING no one has really ever been able to define. Mostly because the don't know how it happens or how to create it.

Some people "feel" lucky and won't buy a lottery ticket unless they have that feeling. But they can't tell anyone else how to feel that way. It runs in some families, particularly among females, but again – there's no particular DNA strand or link or coding that really says what makes lucky people that way. (And if they did, I suppose they think we're going to have some sort of re-coding surgery to "correct" it? Painful.)

What I've known about luck up to this point (and before I tell you about a recent breakthrough) – was two things:

1. You can only "make" your own luck – by positive thinking and pro-active living.

2. The old quote, "Luck is opportunity met with preparation."

And while you can see that these are related, and both quite sensible, they still fall quite short.

• While you can be as pro-active as you want, this means luck is dependent on working hard – and you can work yourself to death thinking as positive as you want and still have horrible luck – even "dying in the traces."

• If you don't know how to prepare for the luck which is supposed to fall into your lap, you might as well stay in school for the rest of your life – because how are you supposed to know what luck to prepare for?

The way I've stumbled on lately seems the most direct route.

I use Levenson's releasing technique.

Of course, this is "Law of Attraction" on steroids. You simply see what you really want out of life and release all the reasons you can't have it, or aren't worthy, or how having it "gets back at" people, or whatever feeling that comes in when you get that concept. You don't push the other feelings away, you just let them go.

Of course, Larry Crane and Hale Dwoskin have their own ways and approaches to get this done. But they are both based on the original Lester Levenson research.

And this really boils down to just getting the effort out of your life – which is really just improving your "luck-ability" score. Anyone you've ever heard about or met wasn't working hard or studying their butts off when that lucky event showed up in their life. They were taking it easy and the luck wasn't even expected.

That's what releasing does. You get all the effort out of your life, and definitely, certainly quit thinking about it.

In earlier posts, I've covered this as "intuitional living" – and now we could actually call it effortless living.

When the person who is luckiest in life firt considers something, they release every thought or feeling they have about it and then lets the Universe bring it to them on it's terms. Like Wallace Wattles said about using the normal lines of industry and commerce.

Sure, there's a few other details to it, like always picturing it in the Now – so you always see yourself as having this already in your life – but it's really simple and easy once you study the basics.

So I invite you to check out the the authors' sites above and put these into your life as continuing habits.

And get incredibly lucky all the time at everything.

The Universe is One Big Joke – and We are the Punchline, not the Butt of it.

THE UNIVERSE CAN BE seen to be one huge joke. And the people still here never got the punchline. Far from being the butt of the joke, they actually started the joke themselves.

For the Universe is built out of limits. We agreed to have limits and so we have them.

I do a lot of volunteer work for an outdoor education center called Scattering Fork. We take small groups out in the woods on what is called a low-ropes course, and have them do team challenges – which make them think and act outside any particular box they are in. I've started telling them that there are 1) the rules for that particular challenge, 2) the safety rules for that challenge, and 3) anything else they want to make up for themselves. The first two sets you have to follow – but you can do whatever you want with the third set.

And it takes awhile before they figure out that they set far more limits than the challenge requires.

That is really a microcosm of this Universe we are in. None of this that surrounds you is serious. Start releasing all the time, consistently, and you'll see this to be true. You'll find yourself calmly cheerful, optimistically expectant for the next thing that the Universe is bringing you.

People who are serious about the world around them haven't figured out what the joke is. And might not for a very long time.

But those who have will just smile quietly and ask you if you need any help with that...

Because that is actually how easy it all is. This world around us is a piece of cake, a cake-walk.

It's not serious, it's a joke. Be the punchline.

How I Get Rid of Nagging Worries and Stress

THE TRICK TO ELIMINATING worry, anxiety and stress is actually easier than it looks.

But it's taken me some months of practice on top of years of study in order to figure it out. And I didn't need any expensive life coaching to help me.

The simplicity is using the Levenson releasing technique to get rid of those continuing thoughts that seem to rattle around your mind and distract you so much.

You just follow these direct steps:

> 1. Accept that nagging thought – let it be. Don't resist or fight it any more.

> 2. Then simply be willing to let it go and then just let it go.

Sure, Larry Crane and Hale Dwoskin have more steps you can use to do this – and you should check them out if you're interested.

But keep it as direct and uncomplicated as possible.

The only refinement I have to contribute is that you don't want to be figuring out why or "how come" or "what it all means". You just want to get to the point that you can accept the thought for what it is and then let it go. Dwoskin was telling me that through his tapes months ago, but until I actually got down to the simplicity of it, I was still looking for symbolic or metaphysical reasons – or considering that something was happening somewhere that I was connected to.

Sure, there might be reasons or explanations or connections to others. But you won't hear about those through thinking about it. In "Go Thunk Yourself, S'more!" I came upon the idea of "Intuitive Analysis" – where you just let your intuition start answering the questions you come up with. It's a much faster and easier way of studying things than most people use. And your intuition, like any muscle or skill you use, gets better and stronger with practice.

Your thinking speeds up incredibly. And your stress drops away remarkably.

But if your thinking is filled with negative, critical, stressful, worrisome, or other useless thoughts – then it's not all that comfortable. The trick is to get rid of those type of thoughts and start appreciating the intuitive and inspirational glimpses you have – and these are always accompanied by happiness, joy, acceptance, courage, and peace.

This is "being in the zone", or better – living in the zone.

You have to get the contra-survival thoughts out of your system. Look at them for what they are and then let them go. Don't think more thoughts about them, just let them go.

If it's peaceful, accepting, courageous – then you aren't really having your best thoughts. And those other thoughts just need to be let go. Like you are constantly working to help everyone around you, even those who have really "ticked you off" at some time in the past. Anyone you are working against, trying to control, or inhibit their success in some way – all this simply works against you. Golden Rule again. You are really just helping everyone around you to become more perfect – or to let their native perfection shine more brightly through.

Just get over those thoughts. Accept them as existing and then let them go. Too easy.

It works for everything. Every time you get some stress on your lines, if you practice just letting stuff go, then it gets easier and easier to live an incredibly peaceful and calm life. Everything goes well for you.

Too easy. And that's why people don't do it. They want something complicated and difficult.

But you can use this today and start getting all worry, stress, and negative emotions right out of your personal life. Right now. Try it and see. And start welcoming your native abundance and prosperity into your life as this "stress management" takes root.

And check out those other authors if you want to know more about how to apply it in your own life.

III – The World is Just as You Create It

All God's Children are Kahunas...

YOU KNOW, WE ARE ALL Masters in our own right. True. Just look inside and you see the perfection that you already are.

The ancient Polynesians had this completely right. Nowadays, when you say Kahuna, you either think of some surfer dude who always beats everyone else out in the competitions – or some mystic healer who can fire-walk, control nature, and maybe raise the dead.

But "Kahuna" always met something like "keeper of the secret", although that is a very loose translation (suitable for us ha-ole's who don't speak a word of it). There were kahuna's for every trade and business and activity. Our use would be "mentor" – as you would seek out these experts if you wanted to learn that skill or art. (Fishing kahuna's, weaving kahuna's, gardening/farming kahuna's, etc.)

And so, originally, there were kahunas all over the place. (Check out Wikipedia for these terms.)

It is even so today. Masters (kahunas/mentors) of any trade actually abound. Our approach with the Levenson releasing technique, is to enable everyone to master themselves as well.

My approach, different from most, is to tell you that you don't have to have a lot of money, or sexual partners, or servants, or impeccable health to be a complete success. You don't have to control vast estates of property and hundreds or thousands of employees to be a success.

But certainly, you need to be free of having to have approval from anyone else about what makes your success.

For the only person who can weigh in on your level of success is you. You either are doing what you want to do in life, or you aren't. And the only one who sets the decisions about what you should and shouldn't be doing is you.

That is the freedom which Levenson releasing technique brings – to be able to be, do, and have anything you want. You don't have to have money or prowess in order to accomplish whatever it is you want today.

If you want to stay at home and home-school the kids while maintaining the household, then that's perfectly fine. So is flying airplanes for a living. Anything you want to do that isn't hurting anyone else or illegal because of that fact – you should be able to simply learn to do as an expert in that field. A Kahuna. A Master.

And any Master of their craft does it with an ease that makes it seem like they were born to do just that. And it's probably true. For when a person is following their passion, it's something that they meant to do since they were born (or thereabouts.) But that doesn't mean you can only have one passion. Many people have several and either master all of them, or shift from one to another, mastering each in turn.

The key point in that is that they do it with ease. That is where Levenson releasing technique comes in. Masters release on everything and anything which interrupts or interferes with their practice of their craft. And they live rather calm, peaceful lives. Even if it's a hut on the beach they have to rebuild every few years. Or if its a stone hut in the glens of Scotland so old that there's no record of when it was first built. Or the business executive who has been rising through the ranks for 20-30 years and stands a chance of being the COO or CEO soon. Or the administrative assistant who has seen those CEO's come and go – but knows how to help them all be a success through her mastery of corporate policy and human behavior.

There are Masters who walk this earth and they need not be famous or wealthy or outrageously lucky.

And the reverse is true. People who win lotteries are often bankrupt and further in debt a couple years later – because they never learned how to manage wealth. People who have rented their whole lives aren't necessarily ready for home ownership. Because a politician is able to get elected due to his great speeches doesn't mean he's ready to be a statesman.

As well, most people are hampered by popular success – celebrities often no longer have any life of their own once they've "made it." So being a quiet success and having everything you could want is just fine with most people.

My point here is that you are looking for personal freedom, above and beyond any fame or fortune. The society around you worships these ego-traps. That doesn't mean you have to.

You have to want freedom more than you want the world. And once you get yourself on that route, you'll walk it right on out. Sure, others may pass you by, or maybe you suddenly attain it in a flash after pursuing it for years and years.

And after you Master yourself, then what? Practically, the release technique has been used to help people become millionaires and resolve relationships, and create huge successes. But the people who only used it for those material things wound up in trouble again, sooner or later. Because money, fame, fortune – all these are part of the World. They are not part of Freedom.

Doesn't mean you'll be broke and lonely – those are also part of this world. When you look for the Freedom, Peace, and Joy which have always lay within you – just waiting to be let out – then the world gives you anything you want. Because you don't need it anymore.

So: become the Master you already are. Let your light shine.

Love and Life Without Limits

YOU MAY RECALL THAT we've gone over this point that all people, all humankind (and this also extends to all life and maybe even inanimate matter according to the quantum physicists) – that we are all connected some how, some way.

The only thing that keeps us separate is our own oddball ideas that we are separate.

And, of course, you eliminate these oddball thoughts by using the releasing technique constantly.

Once you do that, do you know what happens?

Unconditional love.

At that point, there is no one you can't get along with, no one that distresses you, no person or animal which doesn't respond positively when you communicate with it.

Because without all those thoughts holding you back, you are in a state of unconditional love with the world around you.

It's kind of weird, I guess, to think this way. (But you can always release that "weirdness" thought, can't you...)

Our most ancient philosophical and religious traditions hold this to be true. We are all connected.

Which gives another reason for quieting the mind. What you think, others can experience. You can't disconnect or shut down those lines. They are hard-wired, always on.

But you can quiet your mind, constantly release the thoughts that come in. You can live in peace and constant happiness – which is then what you are sending out to the world.

You can express unconditional love to those around you.

Now this doesn't mean you just lay down and become a victim – far from it. In fact, people who can't control their negative thoughts will start to stay away from you. Because they also know that the Golden Rule works regardless. And they don't want to share those negative thoughts with you, as they'll come right back to them.

Of course you can suggest they learn the Levenson releasing techniques. They may or may not take your suggestion. But just keep to your *own* level of internal peace and unconditional love and help them however you can.

Meanwhile, just continue to release any thought that comes in and work for that higher Goal of letting your own Personal Freedom come out.

The world around you will probably calm down immensely. Imagine a board room where all the executives in it were completely calm and in communication with each other. Makes for short meetings, very efficient.

So there is a reason for me to write this, for you to read it, for us to help people find their way to this technique.

See what you can do today to help someone else find their way to this. If it's a hassle, or a problem, then just sit and release on it.

And if you really want someone to find this, then take that as a Goal and release it as happening.

What We Are All After is Both Different and The Same

I'M NOT HERE TO EXPLAIN how the Levenson releasing technique works or to sell you on any particular kind or type. You'll find on this site many links to stuff about Levenson and all the teachers who have picked up his method and run with it.

You won't find a lot of Levenson or the others repeated much here. Reason being is that you need to find out for yourself. And the other point is that it really doesn't matter that much. When you understand the core material of how to release, then it's really simple after that. The hardest point is keeping going right on out.

This world we live in is filled with every reason not to continue and not to regain your Freedom. That Freedom, your own perpetual and personal peace and happiness – they all lie within as they always have. There are far too, too many stories where (like Conwell's "Acres of Diamonds") the person went off searching for something when he already had it right at home to begin with.

And all these teachers are taking the risk of all sorts of alienation and being compared to a scam and so on. Practically, they are just there to help you.

The way each of these various teachers help you is to educate you on the basics of releasing and then get out of your way to let you do it. They each have their systems, but it's no different in its basics.

All the problems, the pains, even the illnesses you have currently can be traced back to something you are holding on to for dear life. Problems are something you had in the past, and those solutions are being forwarded onto your current livingness. That is what all those collected thoughts are for – to simply prompt you with solutions.

However, the solution is the problem. And the only reason what you are facing still exists. Just face it, and let it go. That easy. That direct. Sure, you might have to get rid of an untold number of feelings and what-not thoughts which crop up just so you can then look at the basic scene – but the more you release, the easier it gets.

And that is why you need to develop the new habit of releasing constantly. Plus meanwhile, getting the TV, radio, newspapers, and anything else irritating out of your life. These just hold you back by giving you more to release.

You want to be releasing your basic feelings and thoughts – the ones which are holding you back all the time.

These basic negative-thought-habits can be worked backwards from a couple of ways:

> *Is your current thought or feeling the way you'd like to be treated?*

-or-

> *Does this thought or feeling give me greater peace or happiness?*

If you answer no to either of the above, then just let it go. (But practically, as Hale points out, you want to release all thoughts anyway – since any thought or belief or consideration just holds you back. So release anything and everything that comes up.)

Then, once you get your mind quiet (at least enough so you can hear yourself think), then focus on something which would help you help others if it showed up in your life.

When that appears, get the idea of it showing up. And then release any negative feeling or thought that comes in. Like how it's impossible, or how people won't approve of you, or anything like that (as the taxes you are going to have to pay, for example). Just keep releasing about whatever it is that you'd like to show up until you can hold that idea of it showing up right in front of you easily.

Then simply let it go – and let the Universe figure out how to manifest.

And that's all you do on it. Period. Don't plan about it, don't think or worry about it. Just get the idea that it's completed and present - and then release it

Do that at least once a day. Some do it several times a day.

The rest of your day, you are working to help others – in any way you can. What makes the stuff you need and want show up faster is to help others with whatever it is that they are trying to get into their own lives. The more you help others, the faster your own life is filled with everything you need and want.

And that includes Personal Freedom.

Because the bottom line is that we aren't in this Universe to accumulate toys or other great stuff. You can only take the Love you feel within. So concentrate on going Free and helping others regain their personal Freedom.

The Trick is to Get the Ego to Undo the Ego, the Mind to Undo the Mind

AS WE'VE COVERED BEFORE, the mind and the ego are mostly composed of fiction. You've set up various thoughts as solutions to problems and hold them in place so you have a ready answer to anything that comes in front of you.

Unfortunately, these all have limits on your actual ability.

Thoughts are always, dependably, second to action. Action occurs without thinking. Like your blood circulating and your breathing. Sure, if you work at controlling your breathing, you can lower your heart rate.

To do this you have to concentrate.

To concentrate, you have to shut out other thoughts than the single one you are working on.

The problem is that most people can't do this. The vast majority of people just let those 50-60,000 thoughts a minute just race through their head, willy-nilly. And they try to get them to shut up by watching TV, listening to loud music, drinking alcohol, or taking other drugs – or some combination of the above.

If you want personal Freedom, you are going to have to quiet the mind.

Releasing technique allows you to just let go of the thoughts you've been holding onto and then the mind quiets. It's that simple.

And as you quiet the mind, your ego also tends to start to vanish. You start to look at the world for what it is, which needs very little thought. You can cease to be required to act, but just start watching this fantastic world around us go through its paces.

Sure, you are going to want to help out and do things – but you don't have to anymore. The difference is extraordinary.

You can now live your life exactly the way you've always wanted to – free from others' control, approval, or any need for security. You'll have few, if any, fears – including dying itself. When something does come up, you diredly look at it for what it is and then let it go.

Your ego just becomes a mirror of the world around you – like Teflon, nothing sticks to it. So you can simply start helping out wherever you are needed – or following the intuitive glimpses you receive to fulfill whatever passion you find you now have (which you've had all along, but were too busy thinking about it...)

There is no chance that you will lose your mind or your ego. You'll still be you. But you'll be more you, and your mind will be your own – not cluttered with others opinions of you or fears of what they might think or what might happen to you.

Try it and see.

Just be still for a moment – right now. Take whatever thought or feeling that comes in and accept it, then let it go. And then keep doing it. Funny enough, even if you think it's the same thought – it will be a lesser shadow of that thought, or a slightly different version. And as you keep confronting it and letting it go, it will get less and less.

Once you get releasing down to a consistent tool in your life, your mind will markedly quiet. You'll have more peace in your life, more happiness. You'll appreciate the world around you and have a lot more to give in return for all you've been given.

But you won't get there by just reading this.

Try it for yourself. See what results you can get.

Taking the Easy Way Out to Personal Freedom.

PART OF THIS RELEASING idea is that you are taking the effort out of everything you do.

If all actions you took had no worries, no stress, no concerns, no negative feelings connected with them, how hard would they be to do?

How about having a day off, walking in the woods or along the beach with nothing bothering you, completely at peace? Easy, isn't it?

And when's the last time you were actually able to enjoy such an experience?

Which is why I suggest you get releasing as a constant mental activity instead of thinking.

Just being there in Nature is one of the most enlightening experiences a person can have. Yet most people are worried about where they parked their car, whether their sinuses are going to act up, if they turned off the stove at home, if they are missing a sports game, if that business deal on Monday will go OK...

They aren't just being there and enjoying the moment.

Releasing technique takes care of that.

So when you get all this releasing done, you are taking the effort of out all that you want to do. (Now notice that we are saying "want" and not "have" to do.) Even if someone asks you to help them with something, you can do it effortlessly if you aren't having some thought about how you don't want to be controlled or if they are going to approve of how you are doing it – and so on.

Effortless action.

You really wind up just being able to let go of all your "do-ership" Once you get the mind quiet, then the actions you should be taking just come to you. And almost do themselves. Because you aren't concerned about anything and can simply stay detached and enjoy the peace of the action.

And you'll be filled with happiness. Actually, what is happening is that you are now radiating happiness. Then that helps everyone around you. Who doesn't like to be around a happy person?

But your happiness, your peace – are just waiting to be let out. You start to radiate your own happiness and peace when you quit wasting time on all those internal thoughts which have kept you "boiling over" all the time. You don't want to tell people what you are really thinking, as that isn't the way you'd like to be treated. So you hold it inside, along with everything else.

Where you are only at ease and in full communication with the world around you, then it's easy to just beam out happiness and your own internal peace. And you are a person that is in demand, as people love to share in your happiness and peace. But you really don't care whether or not other people like you – because the secret is in how much *you* love others, how much you can help others, how much you can give.

This open-handed help is the key. When you don't have to have anything, everything you really want or need will show up.

And then you can concentrate on simply going Free the rest of the way.

You'll know when you get there.

How to Take Control Over Everything that "Happens" to You.

RESPONSIBILITY. THAT'S the ticket.

One of the ways to speed up arriving at your Goal of personal freedom is to look over what has happened to you and check to see what it is that you did to cause that. Just hold that idea until the answer comes out of your subconscious (or any other part of your mind).

Then you'll have what you need to use the release technique.

Let's start at the bottom. You can release your feelings and they don't come back when you do. So you are responsible for all your feelings. After all, you recorded and put them there to begin with.

So when you have your feelings all sorted out – those random thoughts which come in and tell you how to feel about any given situation, as opposed to honestly reacting to the situation in front of you – then you can be responsible for creating those feelings which will best resolve that situation.

If you let your thoughts run your life, then you will always be a puppet on a string. Never responsible for what happens around you, never in control, always miserable.

When you take responsibility, you can take control, you can run your own life – be in charge, be confident of the outcome, achieve your goals.

Get into constant releasing, you can calm the mind and so see more clearly and take more responsibility and control in your life. As you do, your world becomes saner, better organized, simpler. Everything you need or want comes to you easier.

The next step after calming the mind and getting the world giving you everything and anything you want, is to answer, "What am I?" The answer to that is the capstone and you'll then have assumed complete responsibility and complete control over your world.

After that, it's up to you what you want to have, do, or be. But by then, you'll also have a really good idea of what those are.

But you won't get there by just reading my writings. You'll have to prove this for yourself. Otherwise, it's just more smoke and mirrors.

Check it out for yourself.

How Does Helping Others Help Me?

HELPING OTHERS IS THE best way to speed up helping yourself. This is a very, very old idea – but it's almost disappeared in our modern "culture". (At least, until Levenson's releasing technique.)

The basic understanding below it is that we are all connected. The fallacy of our modern days, and how this game called the Universe became a "trap" was that the idea that we are all separate came around and got agreed upon.

If we aren't really connected, then it's OK to cause you harm, since it won't affect me, will it? But we had these reminders over and over and over, in every single major and minor philosophy and religious text: what you cause to others happens to you.

One of the most recent versions of this was "Treat others as you would like to be treated."

From this you can also see: "You have to give before you can get."

But it's all back to the point that we are all connected. Consider that old adage, "When you blame someone else, one finger is pointing at them, and three are pointing back at you." True, isn't it?

When you make someone feel bad, try to make them responsible for some situation or outcome, they feel bad, but you feel worse for having done that. Because it really just comes back to you, regardless of your considerations that you and that person aren't connected. Because you are – and down deep, you know it.

The Golden Rule works whether you believe it or not. It has nothing to do with beliefs, which are just thoughts, after all. It's the way this place was set up.

It's not just me saying it – but I tell you again: throw this away and check it for yourself. Watch others' lives and see if it doesn't happen to them like that. Go around cheering people up and see if you don't wind up more cheerful yourself. I don't advise anyone to go around being critical of others, but you probably look back at situations where you could have had a better outcome if you didn't criticize some person at that time.

Whatever you send out into the world comes back the same way. Some world-views hold that it comes back stronger (remember the three fingers above?) Others say it's an "eye-for-an-eye" type of phenomenon.

And so those people who are constantly deceiving people wind up being scammed themselves. And their money goes through their fingers like it wasn't theirs – which is true.

If you look over your life to see how you can improve the lives of others around you, and then take actions to improve those lives – you'll find that your own world improves to that same degree, or more.

So if you have a certain goal, help others achieve a similar goal they have – and then yours comes around that much faster.

And if you are after personal freedom, well...

Again – disregard what I say here and test it for yourself.

IV – Ultimate Freedom is Already Within You...

Not Just a Board Game: Live for Others in Order to Improve Your Own Life

THERE IS REALLY ONLY one way to play the game of life. It's how you win.

Here's the bottom line – we are each individually and personally here to evolve, to get better, to make the best of life in this existence that we can.

Now, despite all the various "Laws" which have come up over the years, there is only one which is observed by every known religion, philosophic, and deep thinker on this planet – from time immemorial up to the present moment. Because it can be proved by every single person to exist and work.

"You only get back what you give away."

And this Law governs all success, all health, all the wants, dreams, and desires any human could expect to be, do, acquire, or attain in any life. It governs everything.

For some, this means "Love your neighbor as yourself." In other, older versions, "an eye for an eye, a tooth for a tooth."

(And there was that famous judge who put an end to the physical interpretation of this by agreeing that they could have their pound of flesh, but they could take only that – no blood or other fluids, nothing else.)

It is the Golden Rule in various versions, the Koran as well as the Bible, as well as ancient Druid texts, Hindu, Egyptian, and even earlier to the oldest philosophies that still survive in remote Polynesian islands.

We are all connected, there are no limits – so this rule says that when you hurt someone else, you hurt yourself, when you help someone else, you help yourself.

If you look at any millionaire, billionaire or better (or worse), you'll see that their money acquisition was on the backs of making other people rich at the same time. Ray Kroc (founder of McDonald's chain) made far more millionaires than he could count. Sam Walton's (Wal-Mart) expanded the sales of his suppliers many times over and was constantly working to improve the quality of life of his customers.

And that is the point to all this. To the degree you want to succeed in business, to get a great amount of income flowing toward you, to have a great home, nice stuff all around you – what do you have to do? What do you have to put your attention on?

The value of the product or service you are giving away.

Now, this doesn't mean we need to all be paupers. Quite the reverse. The oddest thing is that people won't value something, won't really use it, unless they have to give something of value in return. That is really the only reason profitable commerce continues to exist and communism/socialism always fails.

That Rolls Royce or that Cadillac is worth every penny. People will pay more for grass-fed beef which is raised naturally without hormones or excessive growth-producing chemicals – that they know where it came from. They'll pay several times what it took to create that beef and grow it for the two years it took to get to that size. Several times what they could have paid for that same beef at an auction yard and gotten it processed.

The added value is in bringing that specific product to them in a way they can use it best.

That's more to our point:

> *Any business or individual will only succeed to the exact degree that they help others succeed.*

For better or worse, Bill Gates' billions didn't arrive without giving a great deal of value to the computer industry and the personal computer buyers. Us, in other words. Take any industry leader and the also-rans. The best, the top of their class always, always gives value in greater quantity than they extract. Sure, there are "other factors" – but that is the key one. (And why Apple and the Linux community hold onto major shares of this market? Even better value.)

Your own success it really just this point:

> *Whatever it is that you want – help someone else get it, or better, several someone's. If you want help, help others. If you want to get rich, help others get rich. Want better health? – Work to improve others' health.*

There are examples all around of how this works.

The reverse is true – scam other people and you can't hold on to your own money. It's only temporary. If you want permanent wealth around you – you'll build wealth for others many times over in advance of your own, or at the same time. Not afterwards. (ripoff artists and politicians only have to hide when they are hiding something.)

This isn't a government job, which by definition is *always* taking something away by threat of force to "help" someone. I'll dissect government at another time. The deal here: all help is a personal thing. What ever you personally want, you have to help others get it first, or at least at the same time you do. Only then can you really fulfill your desires.

And once you get everything you could possibly want or need? Then just keep helping others learn how to do it for themselves. That's why all the really rich turn to helping others, even giving all their wealth away (like Buffet, Gates, and earlier, Carnegie, Rockefeller, etc.) Because now that you're there, what else do you have to do?

And how about those who amassed great fortunes only to die bankrupt — they didn't follow that Golden Rule. Help others all the time. Every way you can.

That's the only way out of this human existence we share on this planet at this time. Remember, Jesus said that "Heaven is within you." And hell-on-earth is just ignoring this one rule.

Your choice.

How You, Me, and the World Around Us Actually Works

YOU CAN GET EVERYTHING you want in life – and actually do. Whatever surrounds you is already what you've always wanted most.

So if you want something different, you simply have to change your mind.

But how to change it is the problem. Apparently, anyway.

Let's look at basics:

- You exist.

- You create the world around you by what and how you think.

- Your thoughts don't have to be on automatic all the time.

- You can change your feelings whenever you want.

- A thought about something in the future will never create anything – because the future never comes.

- Thinking about the past only changes your ideas about what happened before this point, if only a couple of micro-seconds ago. Those thoughts don't change the Now.

- Only creative thinking about what you want right Now will change what you are experiencing right Now.

• As everything you think comes back to you, thinking destructively about anyone or anything doesn't do or bring you any good.

There are a lot of therapies out there which cost a lot of money, but don't practically do anything (except make that person or organization rich) – because they deal with things that occurred in the past. What happened is done. Over. Kaput. Finished. Finis. You can't change it and thinking about it won't improve what is happening around you. Psychiatry and any of these "sciences of the mind" which deal with regression – all these work ineffectively (and expensively) if at all. And they are always a continuing saga – you have to keep getting more sessions and paying more money from here on out.

The only reason we can't get what we want in life to show up around us is that we are always keeping thoughts around us from the past. Those thought-habits are to keep us safe, to make sure people think well of us, to ensure we can control the world around us.

All those reasons are bogus.

Because the World around you is exactly what you think. Exactly.

Worrisome thoughts create worry and anxiety around you. Fearsome thoughts create more fear. Angry thoughts create more anger. Look around you and you'll see this is true. Someone loses their temper – and suddenly everyone around them is a little more angry, or a little more fearful.

But the reverse is also true. Someone coming into a room with a big smile and lots of great things to say about everyone around them cheers everyone up.

Your thoughts – and the actions these spark – create the world around you.

The trick then, is to get control over your thoughts. Now, in "Go Thunk Yourself", I cover in some detail how various scientists have shown that you can change these mental thought habits by around 30 days of practicing a specific pattern of thinking – and that you can change your attitude just by putting a smile on your face – William James pointed this out around a century ago, and Plato way before that.

More recently, I stumbled upon the Levenson releasing techniques, and found an even simpler way to eliminate those nagging worries, fears, frustrations, etc.

You can actually and effortlessly be happy, peaceful, calm, and act with complete courageousness every single second of the rest of your life. Sure, it takes some work, but it can be done.

Which way would you rather live your life?

Lester Levenson and the 7th step of releasing

I DON'T KNOW WHY, BUT you don't find this 7th step of the releasing technique mentioned in the various Larry Crane and Hale Dwoskin work-ups.

Practically, it's been around as a practice since time immemorial.

Here's what Levenson said in a tape series called, "The Way":

> 7. ***Make your behavior that which a Master would do.***
>
> *Whatever you do, do it successfully.*
>
> *The more imperfectly we work, the lower down the scale we are.*
>
> *The action required to go free is releasing all the obstruction.*

A Master, as we've covered elsewhere, is someone who has already achieved a high state of enlightenment and self-knowledge. And there are more around on this planet than we consider. But that's in an earlier part of this book.

For our use here, it is really that one sentence and the explanation I pulled from his tape – not an exact quote, but close.

People have often used others' examples to compare and contrast their own lives with. Levenson is telling you to simply do what a Master would do.

Of course, you probably have heard that phrase, "What would Jesus do?" – which is completely applicable, just as "What would Buddha – or Lao Tse, or Confucius, or Muhammad, or any other major spiritual leader – do?"

The idea that comes to me, particularly in following Levenson's example above, is that you always work for perfection in every single thing that you do. All actions are professional and give a much greater value than are asked for. Wallace Wattles covered that exact point in his "Science of Getting Rich." Similarly Earl Nightingale covered similar points in his "Strangest Secret" recording.

And so very interesting was a point I first ran into from Napoleon Hill's "Think and Grow Rich" – where he quotes the psychologist William James – that all you have to do is to act the part and whatever you do will take the place of any feeling you are currently experiencing. Be brave, and you are. Laugh, and then you'll certainly be merry.

So that gives us a very practical and pragmatic approach to life. Study up on the lives and teachings of these spiritual leaders – or any Master in any field – and you'll see exactly how to approach life from that viewpoint.

Don't assume their persona, be your self – but make your *actions* those a Master would do. In other words, take all this in advisement, but throw it away if it doesn't let you be yourself.

Because you are already a Master, we are just working out how to let your inner light shine – aren't we?

Try this for 30 days and you'll start replacing habits you didn't even know you had.

And as I write this, I can already see where I can get some more improvement out of this – I hope you have as well.

Getting Your Life in Order – Cleaning Your Room

ALL LIFE REVOLVES AROUND order, prediction, simplicity.

And while I've started revolving my own life around the Levenson releasing technique – amalgamating this into the earlier studies I started so long ago with "Go Thunk Yourself" – there are always so many lessons to find just in living.

The most recent one is that you really want to rid your life of things you are wanting to control, needing to approve, or that require your security. It isn't enough just to release on how these are affecting you – there's also where you are still working to do these on/for others.

These type of scenes are just holding you back.

Of course, this goes back to that 7th step of releasing - living your life as a Master would (which just brings out your own native Master abilities, doesn't it?)

So you can take any of the historical Masters who have lived among us (and some say still do) – or just look within yourself to see how you would like to be treated.

It's that easy. If you are involved in some sort of continuing mess where you feel you have to control someone else's actions or activities, then maybe it's time to let that go. It might mean you don't have to deal with those people any more.

But it will mean that your life gets more direct.

And, like cleaning your room, if you start doing this on a regular basis (as I advise getting your releasing going on a continuous basis), then your life becomes simpler and simpler. You live with far less effort. Which then means that magic and miracles become more and more commonplace.

There's far more about what Lester wrote that needs study and reflection. And I'm sure I'll be continuing this as I move to other projects and blogs about them. For me, those are easy subjects to talk about, much more rewarding than other areas.

But try this out for yourself and see if these make sense. See if you can't work at getting your own life more direct by seeing what complicated subjects you can just drop out of your active life.

How You Can't Win Them All, and Why You Shouldn't Try

WHILE YOU CAN AND SHOULD be willing to help everyone around you – and the Golden Rule says that you almost have to – don't expect that the world is going to immediately turn right around and give back.

There are people, sad as it seems, who are bound and determined to simply continue destroying everything and everyone around them in their way along their own little personal path to self destruction. These are the truly insane among us.

It's not that they can't be helped. Or that they can't get better. Or that they can't actually resolve to improve their lives and eventually find their own route and way to personal enlightenment. They are right now hell-bent on wrecking their own lives, which also then affects how they see and treat people around them.

So you have to be willing to "cut your losses" at some point and move these people off your lines. Actually, they will move off yours if you just let them. I think I've gone over this point before of realizing when you're fighting something and directly quit that action. Like finding out that you're beating your head against a wall – the pain is remarkably lessened when you stop.

At one point I'd been involved with ripoff artists for the around 2 years and finally got enough sense to just quit. It was that easy. They actually wanted away from me almost as much.

For them, it was like a tar baby they couldn't get unstuck from (Uncle Remus – Brer Rabbit – Song of the South). I was trying to get them Justice and help them as much as I could. But all my lectures were going on deaf ears. And when I finally saw their view of life, I could understand why they weren't listening – their view of life was that everyone was out to scam them, so no one was able to be trusted.

They are actually in a state of constant denial of the world around them. They are actually fighting everything that they encounter – scamming is their only defense, since the world is out to get them. If there's a brick wall anywhere near them, they can't wait to butt their head up against it. They can't get away from the ego-trap of making money with Other People's Money – yours. Their "work from home" business opportunities are just a second, low-paying wage-slave job. And now you're working for your credit card companies, too.

But this is just to tell you that you can get these guys off your lines more easily than you think possible.

Again, the Levenson releasing technique comes to view as a tool. The direct steps I use to continually apply this in my life are

1. Look over and confront what is in your life – all thoughts and feelings
2. Accept any part of this (or all of it) that you can.
3. Simply let it go.

Of course, life gets easier and more delightful as you do this. You enjoy life more and your feelings become more intense. You appreciate things around you much better. Abundance, good health, great relationships – all these become common place when you use the releasing technique.

You want to use Levenson's releasing techniques continually in your life. And in doing so, you can achieve incredible states of calmness – beyond any meditation – that will take you through anything life has to offer. Ultimately, it can take you into realms most humankind doesn't get a chance to visit often and where few are able to remain.

But that's a story for another time.

Right now, just help everyone you can, even those who don't want your help. But quit fighting anything and everything. Simply let go of all your "wanting to sort it out" and stuff like that. Invest in everyone around you, but particularly those who want to invest in themselves.

People have to make (or find, actually) their own Peace. Some, sadly, aren't actually headed anywhere near that direction.

So let them go – right out of your life. They aren't looking for you – they're looking for people just like them.

But realize that you did make an impression on them, if only slightly.

And be thankful for the true friends you are finding in greater and greater number around you. Because that is what you are attracting with your releasing.

How Can "What am I" Achieve My Personal Freedom?

TO ANSWER THIS QUESTION, you have to drop using the mind. The mind is really only composed of thoughts. Thoughts are simply collected solutions to problems in the past – hoping that we might run into that problem in the future and have a ready answer to use.

But our mind can't really answer a question. It only poses more questions and analysis and reaction about the original thought – so that thinking is just a series of thoughts strung together in loose association. Unless you think in disciplined patterns, (force your mind to think in a concentrated approach) your mind winds up with thoughts widely different from what you started out.

Extreme examples of this are called, "scatter-brained" and also "paranoid-schizophrenic".

Concentration on a single thought is a time-honored tradition of stilling the mind. And practically, it was the only way to do so before release technique came about.

Concentrating on a particular question or situation allows the mind to still and the answer to come from the Universal. We've covered before about how we are all connected and our thoughts are sent out constantly – well, when you still your mind, you are able to get any answer to any situation or problem you have.

(Again, reject this completely and see if it isn't true for yourself. For all you know, you are being scammed right now. Check it out and see for yourself.)

Napoleon Hill gave an example of Dr. Gates, who would sit in a darkened room with a pad of paper, pen, and the nearby light switch. Gates would only concentrate on what was known about the problem at hand. Once he started getting answers, he would turn on the light and start writing as fast as he could to get it all down. Gates had a huge number of patents on file and was constantly in demand as a consultant to the major corporations of the day.

Meditation is often best done with a single question in mind. Concentrating on that will often give faster results than simply sitting in silence for the same period.

Now, combining a single, concentrated attention on a particular question in alignment with continual releasing of all random thoughts, a calm mind – this allows you to go behind the mind to get the answers from the Universal. The mind doesn't give answers, it gives back recordings of earlier solutions to similar problems. It will take credit for the answers which come – but those answers come from the Universal, not the mind.

The mind is only a pile of *recordings*.

The Universal stores all knowledge and is a font of *understanding*.

And once you answer that question, "What Am I?", then you have a grip on that Universal which will never let go.

But don't take my word for it. Try it for yourself.

The Fiction of Death and Living – it's only Love

LIKE LIVING, DEATH is a fiction – a dream – the Maya/Illusion we are all participating in.

Consider this logic, if you will:

We are all connected, the world is what we believe it to be. Those, of course, come from the very old "Huna" philosophy. And the word "philosophy" itself goes to "Love of what works."

Charles Haanel covered Love as a primal force, meaning that it exists and creates the world around us. Factually, and by extension, we are all Love at our base.

Lester Levenson's big breakthrough – the one which saved his life – was recognizing that Love works best on an out-flow. The more you love others is what brings more peace into your own life.

And this is the unconditional love you can find in pets and the saints.

"Sin" is yet another fiction, developed (like "Money") to improve the control, security, and approval desires. These in turn are based on denial of this central concept that there are no limits, denial that we are all connected and part of a greater whole. Huna shamans (kahuna's) had a harder time helping ha-oles (non-natives) just because so many of these imports brought with them the false data and beliefs that a person could harm another. And so would then tell the petitioner to go and "make amends" as they felt best, then come back to do the next step. Max Freedom Long tells about this in his "Secrets Behind Miracles".

So where to people go when they die? Nowhere – and everywhere. Because death is neither an end nor a beginning. I ran across an old Serge Kahili King article recently where he mentioned that an old tradition held that Living was just a dream – that when you "died" you simply woke up to another dream.

Dreams, of course, are another fiction – including the one you are "living" right now as you read this.

All there is, is Love.

Now some Eastern philosophies, and Levenson found these to explain what he had gone through, hold that God is within all of us and we are all part of God. Of course, you'll see the New Thought understanding there – but you will also see that while Alan Watts tells about this concept being integral to Zen Buddhism, it is also in the teachings of Jesus the Christ.

Of course, this makes sense again, since God is Love.

So you have to learn (or unlearn) to love death.

Because, like any good story, it pulls you along the plot line. Where that analogy fails is that this is a story which has no beginning and no end. Sleep is really an artificial end and beginning point of every day – and the enlightened have traditionally found that sleep was another fiction, that in higher states it wasn't necessary.

But this very fear of death is what drives so many of us. Levenson found that this was the arch-angel he feared through his own life. And brought him to the very real point where his doctor told him he had days, maybe as much as three months to live – only if he went to bed and didn't get out of it.

He really found out (since he still had a very active mind and drive to understand) that he had brought this on himself. In doing so, all that introspective analysis took him right out the top and into an unreality with the world around him. It took him 18 years and moving to seclusion in Sedona before he could figure out what he had done in order to talk to other people about it effectively enough to help them achieve that state for themselves.

I am still on this "path" to resolving this for myself. And you'll see the fallacy of that statement – it is really that I am awakening ever more slowly from the fictions I have accepted on how to live and exist.

By the same token, you can see why I tell you to learn from these other Masters as well (Napoleon Hill, Charles Haanel, Dale Carnegie, Wallace Wattles, Earl Nightingale, Serge Kahili King and Max Freedom Long) – as these all studied widely and consolidated what they understood into simple and practical philosophies anyone could apply for themselves.

Each of these found very successful lives – and succeeded exactly to the same degree that they helped others with their own success.

That explains the fiction of Death. Because as we are all connected, our success depends on others' success.

Now, my living on a farm brings me into a quite different, less sheltered view of death. Farming is surrounded by the challenges of growing things and harvesting. Plants, like wheat and rye, are planted in the fall only to "sleep" during the winter and then rise tall in the spring to "die" about June where their seed can be harvested. If you don't harvest the seed, it plants itself to grow again the next year. Cows live longer lives in general. But you have to weed out your stock much as you weed a garden – otherwise, there isn't enough food for all of them and they will all suffer. Cows live, on average about 12-14 years (hardier breeds live longer). But like dogs and cats, they live shorter lives than humans (who live much shorter lives than some trees like the Burr Oak, which can exist for more than half a century). So just in day-to-day living on a farm you see death on a daily basis – if only in the insects making their way around.

And I would invite anyone to arrange their lives so that they can spend a few months or years doing nothing but communing with Nature. And taking that time to look within and find your Self, to really look at what is, to welcome this illusion around us and learn to appreciate it for what it is.

Because the truth and peace you seek is already present. You only have to quit pushing it away or saying it's not there.

Death is only one manifestation of your own self-imposed limits. I hope you enjoy finding others.

What is Your Path – How do You Find Your Way?

ONE KEY POINT HAS TO be covered here.

Your path is entirely your own. There is only one Way for you – and that is the one you pick out and resolve for yourself.

This idea of using the releasing technique to get everything you really want in life – that doesn't work for everyone.

There are exactly as "many paths up the mountain" as their are individuals in this Universe. There can be no "one way and only one way" – because we are all connected, but completely different.

While all spiritual paths are correct in their basic data, many religions (and governments) go astray because they inherit the same problems their followers have. They think they are separate from everyone else and so they are right and everyone else is wrong.

Needless to say, this doesn't work. Thinking someone else is wrong just comes back to you, doesn't it? Accepting people for what they are, giving them unconditional love – these actions will bring you acceptance and love in return, won't they?

That old Golden Rule scene we've talked about over and over.

The other phrase I'm fond of quoting goes: "No one school has all the teachers." That's from the older Polynesian sayings, which are probably the oldest surviving philosophic system that this planet has. And those islands are amazingly peaceful these days.

While I tell people that releasing is probably the greatest discovery since Fire and the Wheel (right up there with sliced bread and spreadable margarine) – I also have to say that it's not for everyone.

I tell you to throw away all that you've read here and prove it for yourself. That is really, really the only way to find Truth. Because truth is completely personal to you. No two people share the same exact truth.

Of course that explains why no government really works and dictators seldom end their career alive and in power.

The best approach is and always has been to let people work things out for themselves. Let communities solve situations as best they can, groups of communities decide what's best on a broader basis, states to solve solutions based on a broad consensus (if at all) and the national government to simply keep its nose out – excepting only national concerns like defense and safeguarding trade lines.

Every single government employee at all levels could release on having to control and approve anything for the rest of us, as well as only doing those things which would benefit others as they would like to be benefited. But they'd have to quit thinking and start looking to a greater power for solutions outside themselves . Don't hold your breath waiting for this to happen any time soon...

But regardless of politics and government, just work out the optimal solution for yourself.

Whatever your path is – go at it until you achieve your own personal Freedom and everlasting Happiness. We all share one other, common thing – inside, we are all Masters. And we just need to let is shine out through all that we've stacked up on top of it. Do just that for yourself and we all win.

Thanks for listening to all I've said here. Now I'm done.

You can safely throw it all away and write your own book now.

I wish you a great eternity.

So Now You Know Your Path – What's Next?

OF COURSE, I'VE BEEN having quite some fun applying what I laid out at the beginning of this, but there's one more update.

Mostly, just working on stilling the mind has done wonders. But the 1-2 punch of releasing any thought that comes in, followed by asking, "What's that thought coming from?" took me right back to "What am I?"

And that has produced the best results.

While I can't say that the mind is completely stilled all the time, I am having wider and wider gaps in time where there are no thoughts and I can just simply enjoy a very peaceful existence, just "Being the Witness" as Levenson covered so often. Because when you still the mind, in my experience, there's not much choice or reason to do anything else.

It's just natural.

And so this is what is bringing this concept I had earlier of "Intuitionist Living" or "Intuitionist Life". The explanation of this is that you really only live that type of life naturally – but your own thoughts take you out of it and make you effort at any decisions or planning you "have" to make. These "now-we're-supposed-to's" and "musts" and "have-to's" are all really fiction.

They only exist in a very busy mind. Quiet the mind, even a little bit, and their force weakens. Life becomes a calm, peaceful existence. (Or at least more calm and more peaceful.)

The intuitional and inspirational insights which start arriving (no longer relegated to pushing through as thought) are fascinatingly simple and direct. There's no question about them, no rush. There is a great deal of certainty accompanying them – but no dire urgency for them to happen.

I'm sure that if I were in a very action-oriented situation, I'd have faster and more immediate intuitions about what to do next.

But the flow of life is fascinating, even at this fairly low level. I'm sure that as I get used to it, all of this will seem commonplace after awhile. And there will be another, higher level to attain which seems uniquely interesting at that point.

So, as usual, throw this away and forget I ever said anything down this line. If it's useful to you, fine. Certainly, your mileage will vary. Definitely.

But I'm certainly having fun with this and thought to let you know.

V – Think Less and Grow Richer

———

NOW IT'S TIME FOR THE breakthrough which prompted updating this book.

Where We Begin...

OUR U.S. CULTURE (AND that of most western countries) has long ago moved beyond resolving the fear of poverty. Helping people move on from the Great Depression inspired Napoleon Hill to write his "Think and Grow Rich". It's easier now to live a higher-quality lifestyle than ever before.

And yet those same forces are still at work to stoke those fears which created that first Great Depression into a next one (just as they have often succeeded in the past). Meanwhile, other inspired individuals are following Hill's lead – finding new ways to help our culture work through our fears to achieve any amount of riches we could want.

As this book is written, we have more billionaires than ever before, and are on the verge of having our first trillionaire in personal wealth appear. All while billions on this planet still live in poverty. Being uber-rich doesn't make you better than anyone else. You can't buy enlightenment or talent, happiness or love. For each of those millionaires and billionaires, they each still have to face divorces, personal depression, and all our common relationship problems, just as anyone else.

Government, and our "media" (which includes "social media") have no answers for this. They are not in the "solution" business. They each are only trying to sell us something.

And none of our current uber-rich seem interested in Hill's mission to make it more possible for anyone else to make their own riches, starting just where they are. The uber-rich just have more expensive hobbies, like a space race.

Meaning, we are each on our own – just as those very few truly successful people throughout our long history have made their own way. In spite of.

Since "Think and Grow Rich" was first published, more people have learned about goal achievement than ever before. And found that book is more widely useful in getting other riches as well.

People who have achieved personal riches beyond mere money have always "laid up" those riches despite the world around them. It can be done, it has been done.

That singular book Hill wrote has inspired more millionaires to grow rich than any other single book (excepting, perhaps, the Bible). The reason for that is because that 1937 version of Hill's practical philosophy of achievement was so basic and powerful in its approach. The natural principles he discovered and proved are basic to all sorts of achievement.

You can get as rich in money as you want - if that's all you're looking for. Anyone can. But Hill in his last books was realizing that there were many more ways to become rich than just money. He listed eight, in fact.

You probably know other areas of life where you can be richer – relationships, health, family... And one of Hill's last books was entitled, "Grow Rich with Peace of Mind".

And while money can't buy these other riches by itself, the goal achievement materials can be applied successfully in those particular areas as well. You have to start by naming what you think success is in those parts – and then the rest falls in line.

Hill's last version of his practical philosophy of personal achievement material – a course entitled "PMA: Science of Success" – is the most refined, and the most effective, but still falls short of what's possible.

This book takes up at the point where Hill left off. It's a completely new approach to to those eight types of riches – an approach which has traditionally been called enlightenment, among other things. The route to that success is to help anyone to realize that they can be whatever they want to be and have anything and everything they want to have.

The approach here is more like: "how to get to where you know you should be, in spite of the fact that there's no apparent road between here and there..."

I've been working this journey for most of my life. And "Think and Grow Rich" took me just so far. Studying all of Hill's materials and those of his students, including any references they mentioned, took me into into a very high state. Still, I knew there was still yet a higher level to achieve – but all the these books just topped out at a certain point.

What I didn't see at that point was that all these books and material were stuck in the same core problem that they couldn't "think" their way past.

So, I kept looking, kept testing everything I knew. Life was already so much more fun. And I was occupied with lots of adventures. I had all the wealth I wanted, plus started achieving goals in my relationships and friendships. My life was more well-rounded.

Yet something was missing. I was still subject to the various ups-and-downs of existence on Earth. For all the heights of creative joy I experienced in achieving my goals, there were dark shadows that took over my attitudes at times.

My own studies already made me review and re-testing everything I'd already covered. And I narrowed down my studies to just what was most workable to help others get to a high state. However, those shadows were still beyond my ability to vanquish.

Then a friend recommended Rhonda Byrne's "The Greatest Secret". You already probably know her from "The Secret" DVD and book.

The great realization in reading her new book was that Byrne was also running up against blocks to her progress toward higher personal riches. She spent the next decade or so after producing that movie hitting up against some other unknowns – and meanwhile collecting tidbits here and there that at last pointed her to other teachers and their concepts. Finally she put it all together.

And that was the missing piece to the puzzle.

There's a high point that people can achieve through goal achievement material, like those of Earl Nightingale, Napoleon Hill, and the people who studied them. And that is a very high point to reach for most people.

Your successes really don't quit, but all goal achievement material can only take you to a high plateau of being able to get *almost* everything you want out of life.

The trick to that high level is that you can still be left with some varied upsets and bad emotional states that come in from time to time. Having a lot of stuff doesn't mean you're happy all the time. Because buying and having a lot of "stuff" doesn't make you happy.

And money can't buy always-on happiness, no matter how much you make.

With Byrne's book I could see that next level.

So I sat about building a bridge that incorporated her material into Hill's goal achievement materials. So that anyone can cross that remaining shadowy chasm and keep going.

This isn't the first time someone has attempted to work out a simple program – one with practical steps anyone can take to become enlightened, just with the books and materials they have at hand. My research had me study many other authors who have gotten people into very high states with their writings and programs. And by collecting these authors, and consolidating their commonalities, I now know why it's taken me five decades of study to have this breakthrough.

One understanding that came through is that there is no one book, one route to follow that will match every individual on this planet. You will still have to make your own path, to test these materials an internalize them for yourself. That is your journey.

At the end of this book is a short-ish bibliography of the most relevant material I can find in this area. Each are useful on their own. Together, they all add up together to make this bridge.

But you still have to walk it.

As one of our teachers said, "You have to want Freedom more than you want the world." And that's your own personal freedom. Beyond anything this world around us can offer.

Once you take those steps, you can live a different life. It's constant joy, peace, and happiness. Riches beyond measure in every area of living. Your life becomes very simple. You don't get upset by anything. Everything you need and want seems to magically appear. Because you don't "sweat the small stuff" like just making a living and getting by. And you see that everything you've been concerned about during your life – and all these former shadows that haunted you so far – is just "small stuff."

Now you're very, *very*, <u>very</u> rich.

Of course, the second best time to start is now...

Two sides to the "Success" Coin.

THIS UPDATE WAS WRITTEN after a lifetime of work in the personal development field. Some half-century at this point.

Again, it also deals with an interesting problem – that while there were many books on how to achieve any goal or riches, there wasn't a single real, pragmatic path to enlightenment (even after tens of thousands of years that humankind has been working at sorting it out.)

My background is farming, engineering, computers, graphic arts. Practical things. Learned in the actual world, where you are required to get results that are sustainable – or you don't keep that job, since it doesn't pay its way. That job can't afford to keep you if they are going broke meanwhile.

Part of that training involved spending some 20 years in a corporate scam/cult that was supposedly helping people move through their "path to higher states" (except it didn't deliver their promises.) In dealing with volumes of people, a person can get a lot of experience with the humankind condition, as well as particularly keen sense of when someone is touting B.S. as fact.

All this boiled down to Hill's observation that to become a success yourself, you need to study successful people. They all follow natural principles to gain their success. Hill discovered and verified these principles, laying them out in his many books and lectures. But you still have to prove them to yourself.

Success, in general, is whenever you achieve what you set out to achieve. This also goes for manifesting "stuff" such as the things you want to attain, acquire, or collect. That also may include collecting life experiences.

The two sides to this are the material and spiritual. However high on the scale we may rise spiritually, there are still some material limits we have to operate through while we remain on this planet. And vice-versa. Material gains can still leave you missing spiritual progress.

(There are some reports of people achieving personal abilities to discard the natural principles of this physical universe, creating miracles wherever they went, but that is beyond the scope of this article.)

For now, figure that this state of "enlightenment" (also know as "awakened", "illuminated", "satori", and many other terms) is simply where you can exist in this universe without being bothered or affected by what goes on around you. In short, being rich through mastering both sides of that success coin.

Again, this article takes a more pragmatic look at things. We're leaving all the flowery descriptions aside.

Spiritual Sources

WE START WITH SEVERAL active and successful researchers in the 50's, just as Napoleon Hill was polishing his "PMA: Science of Success". Two of note are Lester Levenson and Jose Silva. Each of these individually took very different paths to enable people who followed their training to achieve high results spiritually. And when look up their material you'll see some manifestations they were able to do which are way beyond what is taught elsewhere.

Also along this line, we take a more modern synthesis through Rhonda Byrne's "The Secret", which describes her journey from the point where she was introduced to early 1900's New Thought authors such as Wallace Wattles, Charles F. Haanel, and Thomas Troward. She also went in search of current teachers who were successfully coaching/training people along this spiritual line.

That DVD and book she produced were an astounding success on their own. Because they were based on common natural principles known through recorded history and before.

After producing and writing "The Secret", Byrne continued to research. She applied all this material to herself, and found that despite being able to live a usually carefree life, there were still various negative emotional states that would intrude on her otherwise joyful existence. Even some deep depressions showed up. In one of these, none of the practices she had learned about "positive thinking" had any effect. Only when she realized she needed to quit resisting that chronic depression did she start releasing the power that it held. That depression returned again, later, but with much less power behind it – so she kept allowing it to exist instead of resisting it, and its power eventually abated and never returned.

That incident simply encouraged her to continue her own research, which culminated in her recent "The Greatest Secret".

What she has found is basic, core material.

Humankind, in each of our own individual actions, has been seeking this unknown something in our lives. As mentioned above, several individual authors have left books that outlined their own successes in raising people to high levels. Notable personalities through history have made incredible advances, despite personal sacrifices, and left big shoes to fill.

But they did leave their texts. A rudimentary path that is rugged, but still possible to follow. And we've all been on that path. It is a path toward uninterrupted happiness in our lives.

This isn't what you've been told about "reality". We've been falsely told that there are limits to food, to air, to water, to affordable housing, and so on. And these falsehoods have been repeated over and over throughout our lives so that we agree with them. It turns out that the persons pushing these false claims are themselves doing the most to pollute our air and water, to endanger our health, and to keep their own wealth (and so-called "power") at the expense of everyone else. That has been the model for all of our recorded history. It's then no surprise that this is what the vast numbers of people on this planet believe our "harsh reality" consists of.

Enlightenment itself has been framed as some sort of fairy tale. Based in legends. Fables. Not "scientific".

The breakthrough is in dissolving these personal beliefs, and the mindset that contains them. Limits we've been told about how our mind cannot be solved, that we are the effect of our "subconscious" are just more of those false premises that we've swallowed as fact.

Only our modern times – with all our inter-connectivity – has enabled us to see through their self-serving lies for what they are.

Because that bridge between "reality" and true enlightenment can now be written into shape. We have all the materials to build it. Crossing the chasm which has kept humankind in a slow evolutionary process can now be sped up. It's now possible to enable more than just a tiny few out of each century to reach high personal states. What has taken (by many reports) a lifetime or decades, can now be accomplished in a few months, weeks, or days. All depending on how ready you are as a student, how willing you are to achieve your own personal freedom.

Where many of our true spiritual teachers are no longer with us, at least we have their books, and those of their students.

Goal Achievement Sources

THIS IS THE SECOND side of that "success" coin.

The books and materials on goal achievement have been dealing with the subconscious mind all along. And have various recommendations for handling its influences.

Any failure of this material has been solely due to students believing what their own minds were telling them instead of the material they were there to learn. Nothing has been tested more – with outstanding success stories – than goal achievement materials.

Most modern goal achievement references after the 1930's all trace back to Napoleon Hill's "Think and Grow Rich". There are older references in Wattles, Haanel, and even Troward and his student Genevieve Behrend. More modernly, Catherine Ponder wrote a couple of books based on her lectures about Prosperity. These books are still popular and explain certain symbology of the Bible to teach how to make success in our physical world – again, through mastering control over the mind, both conscious and unconscious/subconscious.

This is what makes those materials so effective. You can see here how these goal achievement methods compliment the spiritual ones. They work together as a unified system.

When you have decided on your goal, the bliss you should follow, then you can start implementing the obvious steps – your plan – and work to permanently remove any of your own mental activities that aren't contributing to that end.

Goal achievement is a simple way to start. Get these materials and master these, implement the natural principles in your own life. Meanwhile, study their related materials, including Byrne's "The Secret" and "The Greatest Secret". Start studying through all these referenced teacher's materials. Do your own work on this. Question everything you read and listen to and view. Decide for yourself what out of this will help you "follow your bliss" and attain, achieve, and acquire everything you could possibly need and want out of life.

Then the game of life becomes a very interesting. And it becomes a game that you win every time.

It isn't the one you've been told about all your life. The arbitraries you've been told to believe don't necessarily work. Find the natural principles, both spiritual and material, that work all the time, every time.

Then your journey to your own highest levels of peak performance will become simpler, more joyful, more peaceful, and more abundant.

You will be rich in spirit and also in the actual world.

Now you know where the real discussion begins. And where we can each individually wind up.

Getting More Than You Need or Want - Except Happiness

ORIGINALLY, THIS CHAPTER was titled down the line of, "Now that you have all this stuff, how come you still aren't happy all the time?"

Because the trick is that money doesn't buy happiness, and all the gadgets and things it buys don't give you more happiness either.

America and the world, for many centuries, has been suffering from a fatal addiction.

It's called *compulsive thinking*.

In the one nation that has the "pursuit of happiness" in its founding documents, our own freedom of creative inspiration has led to the highest standard of living anywhere on the globe, as well as raising many other nation's standards. Those freedoms enshrined in writing have resulted increased wealth throughout our history as a nation.

And that increased wealth also made it simpler to buy things – because not only are we more productive individually, but we produce a lot of things to buy. While other nations have bare shelves, America is known for having an overabundance. Nikita Krushchev found it hard to believe that all stores in the U. S. had full shelves and no waiting in long lines for scarce items. He had to be shown several different stores before he dropped his suspicions that he was being shown staged photo-ops. But his U. S. S. R is no more. And there are now more millionaires in Russia than ever before.

Because they just partially adopted these Western ideas of enabling people to act on their own inspiration to provide high-value goods to those around them, and get rewarded for their work.

Unfortunately, this abundance of material goods and income can still give us problems.

One of the leading copywriters of our age, Eugene Schwartz, explained that the normal growth of marketing brings multiple competitors in each area, and eventually the buyers wise up and realize that there isn't much difference between the various brand names for the same commodity. Schwartz' then said that the solution is to market your produce in terms of *identity*. So we had "Marlboro Man" and "Virginia Slims" woman, as well as "Joe the Camel" - all selling their very similar cigarettes in different packaging and advertising to offer people what they *wanted to become* in their lives.

And that approach made these sales increase for those brands. Its still an effective advertising tactic.

You can see the same thing in carbonated soft drinks. They sold drinks that are actually quite unhealthy – based on the idea of being young and carefree as a sales campaign, but assisting a global "outbreak" of obesity. So much competition came into that area because of their success that the Coca-Cola company started investing in fruit drinks and bottled water – as people started wising up about what they were actually being sold. The sales trend started moving toward healthier products, and the businesses "diversified" to ensure they could also profit off those purchases.

Fast foods also abound, as it's more affordable to simply go out and eat than buy and prepare food in our own kitchens. And these foods also contain addictive substances (salt, sugar, fat, MSG) and are marketed to make us "feel good" about who we are.

None of that really addressed the spreading problem of obesity in both America and worldwide.

The root problem is still our own identity issues.

We want to consume and surround our selves with material goods that display to others what we are – that we are like them and also in that crowd.

The richest neighborhoods and the poorest ones both have one thing in common – these occupants are all living from hand-to-mouth, only a month away from being on the street. No real savings or investments if their job disappeared.

We still very much run off our "wants" of security, approval, control, and belonging – all layered above the fear of death, which is at its base the absolute denial of any identity at all.

That's what happens at death, as we are told by our scientists. Because our "science" tells us nothing can be proven about what happens after body death. And so – we might as well "get all we can while we can."

All because we are constantly being told what our identity is. Told in terms of what we aren't, what we can't have, and that limited amount of time that each of us have to exist on this planet.

We have accepted that we are a body, that we are controlled by our ever-present mind, that we are a personality identified by our name and our skin color and our body's heritage – as well as all that "stuff" we buy.

I only bring this up to remind you that we've already solved these limiting factors over and over in our various philosophies and religions. Thousands of years of solutions all mostly ignored

But as you and I are surrounded by people who consider that we have to rely in "scientifically proved" facts instead of our own direct observations, so many of us keep falling for the same faulty arguments. And the trap never opens for those.

In earlier books, I mentioned an "awakening" incident that happened to me one day. I was on vacation on the family farm and was out in the woods one day, walking with the two farm dogs. Then suddenly all thought dropped away. Only peace remained. I still don't know how long I stayed in that state, since there was no evidence of time passing. But the sheer surprise of achieving that effortless state stuck with me.

I was later able to replicate that state anywhere on the farm, any time I wanted. Later, I was able to experience it in the middle of Los Angeles with it's constant traffic, smog, and sirens.

Where I was didn't have to affect what I thought or how I felt.

And since I was working for a "self-help" corporation at the time, I quickly saw that what they were promising "anyone could achieve with their programs" didn't actually cover that improved outcome I'd experienced. Their programs stopped short. That was the beginning of the end for me working there.

That event also was the beginning of the next two decades of search for an explanation of how that happened and how to expand it.

THE CORE MATERIALS to getting everything you want out of life are pretty much the same points through all goal achievement materials. Because most of these either say the same thing, which is derived from Napoleon Hill's life long study of successful people. His passion was finding out the natural principles which successful people used to create their success. He was interested in finding commonalities these people used that showed up regardless of where they were located, what education they had, how rich their parents were, or any supposed cultural limitations or advantages.

Hill's drive was to develop a "practical philosophy of personal achievement. As such, it was not a study of what specific marketing or sales programs people followed, but rather what principles were touted by successful people. It wasn't a collection of "how-to's" as more as a collection of "how comes". These were principles that had worked all through history, in all our cultures. The more principles people knew and applied, the more successful they became.

Hill is mostly known for his "Think and Grow Rich". And again, this one book has reportedly made more millionaires than any other single book other than the Bible itself. Countless successes trace their own success to finding and internalizing that one book.

It's not the only book that he wrote. And his later books tend to reveal the improvements he made as he polished that practical philosophy. While Hill's 1937 classic had 13 principles, his books both before and after this had up to 17 principle. A little-known work, titled "PMA: Science of Success" was originally built as a course for insurance salespeople and managers. This contains the final, most polished version of Hill's work.

In that program, you'll find where Hill disclosed his own methods of researching this material, what he did to find the natural principles which govern success. Each principle individually is pretty much common sense. Together, you can see where a person who implemented these in their own life could not be stopped from getting anything they set as a goal for themselves or their company.

Goal achievement material incorporates learning to control your mind, particularly the subconscious. This is the necessary stepping point to discovering your own identity and achieving personal freedom.

By the end of these studies, almost regardless of whose program you study, you'll be able to be and have anything you want. The world, much as "The Secret" teachers disclose, becomes a sort of shopping basket, where you can get anything you decide want to show up for you. That was Rhonda Byrne's introduction to that very wide world – and what led her to studying and distilling an even greater secret.

The trick was that she had to realize that all that ability to get anything she wanted still didn't promise she was going to be consistently happy meanwhile.

Actuality vs Reality

WHAT YOU ARE TOLD IS "Reality" doesn't match up with the actual world you know exists. That actual world is the one where you envision a result and it manifests for you. Like you learn in all the goal achievement materials.

This becomes simpler and easier the more you work with it.

And I'd gotten to this point in my life. A reclusive life on a farm had brought me many benefits. Like Thoreau and Emerson. However, this led me to become more reclusive as a solution to removing nonsense emotions from my life – ones that took me away from peace and tranquility.

But I was still connected to the Internet, which I considered I could turn off at will. Little did I know...

Politics is a downer, no matter what. It's a zero-sum game, which means someone always loses. And any agreement that becomes big enough to pass as a law has parts that both sides disagree with.

And the tumultuous results of the recent American Presidential election turned both sides sour.

I was struck with how involved I became in this. By then, I'd spent my two decades working in finding, studying, publishing, and distilling works on personal freedom (which saw this and many other books released) and – as part of this – goal achievement.

Somewhere before that election cycle began, I saw that my life had become one of ease. I had a steady, independent income and worked from home. The farm I also ran part-time was becoming known for its distinct brand of gentle cattle, while the farm itself became more sustainable and no longer required external income sources to pay its own way.

More than that, I'd found that things were simply starting to appear in my life without effort. I'd follow my inspiration more closely to do certain things, and would find that something appeared for me just as I got an idea of something I wanted.

And yet, I found myself occasionally perturbed, and even incensed at times. The rest of my life was going better than ever before.

So, why was this?

I continued studying and researching. And even committed to a three-year project of teaching myself to write and publish fiction. At the end of that time period, I'd published hundreds of original fiction books. Which, according to Wikipedia discussions, made me eligible for inclusion on their "prolific authors" page.

All that writing project proved was efficacy of the material I'd uncovered and studied on goal achievement. There were natural principles at work that made my success.

But, with all this success, where were these unwanted emotions still coming from?

According to most of the books I'd read, these emotional programs existed because of my subconscious mind. But even while applying the recommended practices those books prescribed to reprogram it, "following your bliss" in life was a hit-and-miss proposition.

Even though I developed methods to to re-train my thinking into a positive mindset, the source of the upsets and angst still remained, just now re-channeled – not resolved.

I hadn't discovered how that momentary "endless peace" I'd found was still being interrupted with these intermittent emotional spikes of irritation.

When my friend recommended Bynre's "Greatest Secret" book, this filled in gaps so the material on releasing and goal achievement joined seemlessly. It was the keystone I was missing.

UNDERLYING THIS GAP was the problem where people don't understand the differences between metaphors, symbols, and facts.

An earlier documentary of Joseph Campbell's "Hero's Journey" showed Campbell retelling an experience of his where he was on someone's TV program, who's host insisted right from the beginning that myths were lies. Campbell replied, "No, they are metaphors."

The host never budged through the entire program. It was an impasse. Toward the end of the show, Campbell asked the host, "OK, give me an example of a metaphor." The host hemmed and hawed, and finally said through his own embarrassment, "The man ran like a deer." Campbell replied, "No, a metaphor would be 'the man is a deer.'" To that, the host retorted, "That's a lie!"

There were now just seconds left to the program. Campbell evenly replied, "No, that's a metaphor." And on that, their interview ended.

In his ever-popular PBS series "The Power of Myth", Campbell explains how religions go off-track when they seek to find scientific and fact-based explanations of their own texts – something that would explain how what that text said could be "scientifically" proved. While the existence of historical figures can be proved, even the locations and objects such as Noah's Ark, the more mystical phrases cannot be given that treatment.

You have to be facile in discovering and interpreting both metaphors and symbols. And that is how more millionaires were made by the Bible than any other. Metaphors and symbols also explain the resurgence of "faith healing" in the 1920's, and the rise of Christian Science. The results were there – but couldn't be explained in "scientific" terms as to how they were produced. Because the results weren't reproducible from one person to the next. Healing by faith isn't as simple to explain as Newton or Galileo demonstrated the existence of gravity. Or as a pastry chef can produce the same delicious dessert from a recipe as someone in another country.

Because science has long ago weeded out spiritual explanations. They developed a peer-review process for all experiments that were strictly based on only physical inputs.

Given that, many practices such as the Silva Method, Levenson's Releasing Technique, and Transcendental Meditation all have produced reproducible physical benefits through their practice, as shown through various university studies. Science can't defend their explanations of why it works, but they can prove that many different people can train to deliver the same benefits from those practices

Science cannot explain miracles that seem to obviate natural laws. That the miracle occurred, isn't in question – at first. Just how it was accomplished. And so, there are science "deniers" that then say that because it couldn't be reproduced, the miracle then couldn't have happened in the first place.

But was that historical miracle a symbol or metaphor? Did that modern miracle *not* really happen just because no one can explain *how* it happened? (Actually, that's the meaning of the word "miracle".)

Campbell points to the existence of several myths occurring in recorded form, by peoples in widely-separated continents, who were not in communication with each other. Various scientific theories were held as to how this possibly could have happened (such as migration and intersecting trade routes). Yet they cannot contest that the stories were so similar in different languages, in various continents.

Campbell pointed to Jung and his archetypes, that their may be some psychic or spiritual phenomenon at work beyond the understanding of Science. But he leaves it there. Because his job was to compare these myths, not explain their origins.

When you apply Silva Methods to this area, you can see how such a spread of ideas across continents almost simultaneously was possible – but you still have to understand Byrne's book to put these different elements together in the same body of data.

JOSE' SILVA HAD TO leave school at an early age to support his family. Selling newspapers and shining shoes were early efforts. These led him to work for a barber who had an incomplete electronics home-study course. Silva finished this for him, in exchange for the diploma that the barber wanted on his wall with that barber's name on it.

In a tour of duty in the Army, Silva was introduced to psychology by way of his military training. And while the first set of training gave him a thriving business in electronics repair, that second training also whetted his curiosity about the human mind – which was identified by it's brain waves, that were measured electronically.

Silva's lifetime of study proved the impossible – healing by meditation not only possible, the skills could be taught to anyone.

His late-life studies also opened the door to many psychic abilities, which improved the early studies of Dr. Rhine in MIT. Again, anyone could practice and attain for themselves.

Our use of this is in combination with Levenson's releasing, where a person could readily "tune in" to a meditative state and then release the cause of emotional stress quickly and permanently.

Again, this gets you only so far – even though that combination is farther above most self-help studies. They stil leave you *only* feeling good *most* of the time, yet still able to experience extreme dark emotional states at other moments. Those erratic problems, worries, and others still had to be addressed.

Of course Levenson got beyond these. So it could be done.

Yet something was missing. And Byrne did her own studies, assembling many various teachers over a decade of research. All to provide the missing key: *you are not your mind, you create your mind.*

The mind itself is composed of thoughts. And the purpose of thoughts seems to be manifesting things in our common physical universe.

Daddy Brea, an Hawaiian kahuna and also Christian, considered late in his life that the three minds that Huna teaches are more likely metaphor. This concept is that your conscious mind you control, and can utilize the subconscious mind to access data from the Infinite Intelligence (which some refer to as the super-conscious). Taking the three minds as a metaphor, Huna teachings now explained faith healing and even Silva's success with Remote Viewing and Influence.

Byrne brings the teachings of Levenson in line with other teachers, such that the common conclusion that not only is the mind not the identity of the person, but it's not necessary for living life well.

This then finally explained the phenomenon of the mind seeming to "drop away" and be still, leaving only a "peace that passes understanding." Many metaphysical schools, such as New Thought, refer to "seeking the Silence" to achieve that result.

Byrne's continued studies developed extremely simple techniques that don't require repetitive affirmations to re-train the subconscious. You simply release all thoughts, as well as their resultant negative feelings.

Here, any person is able to now achieve what's been described as an "always-on" meditative state. The results of this are a constant state of joy, of peace, of happiness. Gone are the assorted worries, fears, depression, and so on that are the result of having and feeding a mind.

It's not that you can't think thoughts, or have feelings. You do find, however, that these aren't necessary for living, as they just distract you from Nightingale's "calm, cheerful expectancy" as a way of life and daily living.

This is also an explanation for the New Testament advice to "pray without ceasing."

Are we then touching on something that is another psychic link common to humanity – as the appearance of recurring myths in various different cultures as Campbell recognized?

The World Becomes What We Think – or Not

NOW, AT THIS WRITING, I am not going to claim that I've more than just started on this new leg of my journey. But I can now explain a lot of metaphysical symbols and metaphors in terms of my fiction writing studies.

That three-year study of what people most like in their fictional reading entertainment had as a by-product the study of the human mind through its emotions. Separate to this, I have written up the craft of writing in terms of Campbell's "Hero's Journey" and Chris Vogler's point that good stories are cathartic for the body, as they create a physical response through the glands.

The body, in this case, is your indicator of whether the story is effective entertainment. How does it react to a story you're reading or a movie you're watching. How is some music and dance is so uplifting.

But further than that, where the horror writer Stephen King in his "On Writing" states that "stories are alive" and you are simply writing them into existence.

While there are mystery stories (of which horror is a subset), romances, and adventure tales – these are not "good" stories unless the main characters are also coming to grips with some sort of resolution to their flaws. In short – redemption.

Each of these three main story structures above are judged in Western stories as being good as long as the hero/ine wins out.

In Eastern stories, it's common for the heroes and heroines to die at its end, but only after learning something valuable – taking another step on their journey to redemption.

William Wallace Cook, in his classic text "Plotto", simply stated that there is one basic plot for all stories – *achieving happiness*. Beyond that, his book laid out various ways to generate tens of thousands of unique plots, all based on that one concept.

"Happiness" remains as the one common concept that is the core motivator for popular literature.

Fiction is then a method for people to share lessons as well as get release from the "seriousness" of day-to-day living.

People identify with the main characters in stories as having their own ills and life problems. Gone with the Wind, Dr. Zhivago, Star Wars, Twilight, the Harry Potter series – name any over-the-top sales-chart-busting classic or modern fiction book and you'll see these commonalities.

Top-selling fiction books can describe our own lives in painful detail, but in exotic settings and fantastical problem-solving scenarios.

So we can "escape" and learn at the same time.

All we are doing is to turn off our "mind" for awhile and let the entertainment remind us that what we endure through all our mental thinking in "real life" is just covering up what we natively are – happy, joyful, at peace.

Byrne refers to the result of this human native state is felt as ever-present happiness.

She also explains that this state itself, (which she calls simply "Awareness" is referred to by many names in different philosophies and religions, among these is "Infinite Intelligence".

Again, our "three minds" is indeed a metaphor. Because once you get rid of any need to have a mind, the subconscious mind *as we know it* no longer exists. (This isn't to say that the autonomic-reflex functions that govern breathing and blood circulation don't continue to exist. The explanation here again goes to Campbell, who referred to its existence as a "body consciousness".) It's more likely that we have assigned memories to our cells and thought-patterns are superimposed on the body itself. (Consider the studies of "holographic memories" imprinted on cells. It's as good as any other theory.)

Of course, all this "figuring out" is simply creating more thoughts, isn't it? Assigning more thoughts and feelings to something won't change the result.

The point is that we are not our body, and don't have to take that identification as our self. We are not our name – that's not our identity. And we certainly aren't all the stuff around us that we've acquired over a lifetime of living. None of these are our personal identity. Our pets, plants, and body are alive, but that isn't our basic self. Each of us, in Byrne's term, is "Awareness". We are aware of things around us, but we are not them. Just as they are not aware of us.

Byrne goes on to clarify how that works. As when we quit feeling sad, then we aren't sad. No matter how many times you have said, "I'm sad." Or "I'm upset". Or "That makes me angry."

None of those are your identity. Once those temporary feelings have left you, they didn't change who you are.

All those feelings are just on top of your native state of joy, peace, happiness. You have to spend a lot of mental energy to hold onto those bad feelings. But when they are gone, you return to feeling happy – unless you put some other bad feeling there. Emotions and beliefs are more habitual in nature – but they are still mind-based.

One common solution is where people, especially salespeople, will reprogram their "mindsets" into being positive ones. Because that will get more sales, as you influence those around you to simply drop their negative thoughts and feelings and glimpse at their own native happiness for awhile.

You smile in response to someone else's. But if you develop the habit of smiling at everyone you meet, then you'll tend to drop the other feelings that are making you feel any other way. Because smiling is being happy and being happy is your native state.

It's not a much larger step to simply become aware of that feeling as different than what you now know as being your usual "self". And simply let that bad feeling go.

Byrne's method, as told her by several of her teachers, is to "welcome" that thought instead of resisting or layering another thought over the top of it. Once you welcome a thought, it loses power and will dissipate. You no longer resist anything being the way it is. You welcome something just as it is. You're no longer affected by someone else being upset, or someone acting-out a destructive feeling. You're just being yourself, which welcomes all experience as simply another experience to enjoy.

None of this keeps you from writing good fiction. Because at this native state, you are now in full contact with "Infinite Intelligence". We've had a word for this all the time – Imagination.

Dorothea Brande has excellent advice for people to get inspiration for the stories they are working on: do dull, physical routines such as long walks in the countryside without talking to anyone. Scrubbing floors. Doing a tall pile of dishes. Somewhere along this line, you get an idea "out of the blue". Because your mind quit hiding it from you when you quit using it for a moment during boring, repetitive tasks.

And that is the whole point. Practicing welcoming (releasing) anything that doesn't add to your native joy, abundance, happiness. All welcoming does is give us a refinement on releasing, that goes beyond releasing any fear of death after you've released all known wants. Welcome anything and everything that comes along after that point.

This then makes the world around you into a much simpler place to live in.

And you can imagine how long an angry person could keep up that facade when faced by a group of people who just kept smiling in response to anything he said.

THIS IS THE ANSWER to why there was a difference between Reality as we are told (repetitively) exists, and Actuality – where you call the shots.

Nightingale found a phrase in the back of Hill's "Think and Grow Rich" that formed the backbone of his "Strangest Secret" Gold recording:

> *"We become what we think about."*

And he found that one phrase has come up through the ages in different forms. Much as various cultures came up with the same symbols and themes in their myths, this one idea has racketed through the ages. Each person who discovered it thought, for a while, that they had been the first to recognize it.

Separately, beyond recorded history and surviving by being embedded in a common Polynesian language itself, Huna is known for seven principles, the top one being:

"The world is what you think it is."

These two are subtly different, yet so similar as to be identical.

Both are common in their use of the word "think". But that word has a broad application these days, and is non-specific.

And here you see how Byrne's collection of material on enlightenment then gives us a breakthrough.

You could use other terms to replace the word "think" but most mean you are still creating thoughts.

Try using the word "create", or "love", or "enjoy", instead.

> *We become what we enjoy.*

> *The world is what we enjoy.*

(Interestingly, one of the other Huna principles is "Love is to be happy with." Serge Kahili's talk on these seven principles is included below for your continuing studies.)

What is more interesting is how we might be able to start helping people become enlightened all around us. And quit having the "emotional issues" that are so common today.

Because they quit "thinking" themselves and their world into existence. They start simply enjoying it, instead.

And their attitude becomes infectious to the people in their vicinity. Which reflects in their decisions and actions.

Chop Wood, Carry Water

THERE IS A QUITE FUNNY joke that is at the very beginning of the Tao. The author starts off by saying there's no name for this, there's no way to describe it – and then goes on for the rest of the book trying to describe and name it.

Because the Tao (literally "The Way") has to be experienced to be fully understood. And a lot of that book deals with defining what you are not more than what you are.

Byrne referred to that native state of beingness as "Awareness". You'll need to probably name it something else - as you fully understand apply it in your own life and expand on your success.

The point of continual success to any life is, per Joseph Campbell, in following your bliss. And you already know what this is.

The title of this section comes from Alan Watts, who quoted an ancient sage in this saying, "Before enlightenment: chop wood, carry water. After enlightenment: chop wood, carry water."

Watts explained what he had uncovered in studying the lives of Zen Masters and their students. Monks who had spent years in the monasteries achieved their own "satori". And then they often returned to the world outside – to take up their earlier professions. The farmer returned to farming. The carpenter returned to wood working. And one who had been a prostitute returned to that "oldest profession".

As pointed out earlier, it can take months or years, or lifetimes to gain enlightenment – or just an instant.

And what then?

More than likely, before you took up your studies and disciplines to get enlightened, you already knew what gave you the most joy in your life. And you had invested in learning the craft of that work.

Sure, you now have complete access to all your imagination can bring your way. And yes, you have no limits and can be and have anything you want. Everyone is learning constantly, so picking up a new craft or skill can always be done.

T. Harv Eker pointed out that the graduates of his Millionaire Mind training often found out that once they had acquired the huge home and all the expensive items that goes with it (as well as the maintenance costs), they would downsize into something smaller that "fit" them better.

Dr. Thomas J. Stanley in "The Millionaire Next Door" found that the bulk of the millionaires in the U. S. do not live in posh, gated neighborhoods. Instead, they lived in modest homes in suburban areas.

You don't have to go on stage as an inspirational speaker, or start writing books. You can just do what you most love doing and know how to do. Lead by example.

If you love making things out of metal, and are highly trained as a machinist, wouldn't it make sense to use your skills and aptitude to help people doing just that?

And wouldn't it be a simple life to be able to deal with people in your everyday life who were always full of joy and honestly wanting only to help you achieve all you could?

Serge Kahili King points out that the term "kahuna" is used to refer to anyone who is highly-skilled in a certain area. Whether this is fishing, sailing, building, gardening, or anything. Not just as the TV and movies made that term popular in competitive surfing. Or our books on Huna only refer to those who are experts in what our Western world calls "psychology" or personal development.

Your bliss is what brings you joy, and it intersects with all the training you've done through your life to learn various skills.

Certainly, there would then seem to be a lot more people who had achieved their own high state, and who are simply living normal peaceful lives. Going about their living without standing out or causing a fuss about things.

As the numbers of successful writers and content producers are few and rare, it's unlikely that the majority of people who are enlightened write or talk about it much.

When we review Abraham Maslow's last addition to his "Hierarchy of Needs", we see that the top level is comprised of people who only exist to help others. And that is their "peak performance" skill turned fully on, and utilized freely in their daily work for others around them.

We can also pull from Jim Rohn, who is known for a phrase, "You can get everything you want out of life, if you help other people get everything *they* want out of life."

This is the point: you can have all the peace, joy, and abundance in your life – and live as simply as you want. All while doing what you've found is a way you can help others achieve what they want.

Many older writings and teachers refer to this world as a dream. And that is a simple metaphor. If anything, it could mean that you shouldn't take life any more seriously than if you wake from a dream. Just because you've achieved enlightenment doesn't mean this world we live in disappears. So these "natural laws" or principles still continue to have application in all of our lives. Gravity still works. Air flow pressures still keep airplanes flying. The Golden Rule still exists and can be proved, much as Cause and Effect.

It's just easier now. Because the better you get at manifesting your enlightenment, the more joy and peace and abundance show up in your life – and those around you. Just as you continue to work with others to get these manifesting in theirs.

Chop wood, carry water.

How Does This Make You Richer?

BECAUSE YOU CAN SIMPLY have things appear in your life whenever you want or need them. You only have to define what you consider "rich".

Again, Napoleon Hill gave a short list of different ways you could be rich in your life, and the last one was "sufficient income to accomplish your stated goals."

J. B. Jones made a thorough study of Napoleon Hill's "Think and Grow Rich" and it's background materials when he was a part-time lecturer for the Napoleon Hill Foundation in the early 50's. He gave a short list of references in his own bestseller "If You Can Count to Four..."

Jones' book was written and published near the culmination of a practical business test, where he borrowed $10,000 (in 1950's dollars) and turned it into a business that was earning over ten million dollars of income in just under five years.

The key part of his success system is in the first chapter. He lists four points that are necessary for you to become whatever you want to be and have whatever you want to have:

1. Decide what you want in all it's details.

2. Pretend that you already have it.

3. Say "Yes" or "No" to any inputs you receive from others.

4. Pay attention to ideas "out of the blue" for inspired action.

We'd refine this using what Byrne has provided:

a. Envision your ideal for anything you may find you need or want in your life. Get all the details to it.

b. Consider that need or want already fulfilled. Then welcome that envisioned idea and release it.

c. Welcome all inputs about this as they appear in your life.

d. Your inspiration of action steps to take will appear – implement them as best you can, starting now.

You can see that this is far more direct, and so – more powerful. As you practice these steps, you'll get more efficient at your manifesting. Anything and everything you could possible want or need.

Meanwhile, your life becomes more joyful, happy, peaceful, simpler.

And you can use those four as questions to make decisions as changes enter your life:

- Will this make my life simpler?

- Will this bring me more joy?

- Will this find me more peace?

- Will this help me enjoy more abundance?

Because life is what you make it, just as you create it.

We are all natively abundant. As the Huna principles say, "There are no limits." Any limits you may be experiencing can be welcomed – and released. Because they only exist as thoughts, feelings, and beliefs that you agreed with sometime earlier.

You can be whatever you want to be in life. You can have whatever you need or want to have.

And this can be an always-on ability.

Naturally. Natively.

Core Ideas and Side Benefits

THE ADVANTAGE TO BEING enlightened, over being your average human, is that nothing bothers you. Not "nothing seems to bother you", but nothing actually does. There's this experience that seems to go from calm to joyous, but never the downsides of being caught up in a pure emotional funk that overrides everything else – if only for seconds.

Time to the enlightened is living in eternity. Humans who are tied to time as a "thing" have multiple problems connected with this fiction. Of course, this is where you get into the Zen concept of "there is only now". Huna principles have this as "Now is the moment of Power."

Releasing is letting go. It's also called "welcoming" by Byrne – which is a simpler explanation of how it works.

You take responsibility for your own creations. And any negative emotional thought, feeling, or emotional state is just you denying that somehow you created that.

Resistance is trying to negate or counter-create something in your life. And that's where your failure begins. All of your failures.

Arguing or negating only creates a compromise set of feelings. Nothing is ever resolved. Similar to how Byrne says that "letting it all out" doesn't work – because the underlying thoughts, feelings, emotions all still remain. You have to release them, to welcome them.

You have to start back with the creation itself. And return to a native state of creativity, imagination, intuition. However you conceived that idea to begin with – before you turned it into an automatic "thought" that you could "remember" from time to time.

Once you return to being responsible for your mind(s), then you can see past the metaphor of "having a mind" and return to your native state.

All you're doing is cleaning house. You've attracted and attached various thoughts to various activities, and these have become habitual thought processes – which is a mind, which are emotions.

Emotions are pre-programmed responses, below these lie feelings. And thoughts create most feelings. Not all. Because feeling good is native. But anything other than enjoying everything around you is something you invented – or agreed with.

Again, how you experience the world around you can be examined against four criteria:

- Does this make my life simpler?

- Doe this enable me to enjoy live better?

- Does this bring me more peace?

- Does this manifest more abundance in my life?

Sure, I've laid out lists of books and materials. I've mentioned long programs of study, distilling these to simple points.

While I could write a long and dull textbook on all these things, that wouldn't be enjoyable for either of us.

Your journey is your own.

But we'll meet up again somewhere along the way.

Mindless Goal Achievement

BY THIS TIME, YOU CAN see the joke in that above title. Goal achievement is a native ability all people have – if they know and apply the natural principles in this area.

The trick is that the mind and thoughts just get in the way. And most of these goal achievement materials have techniques to get around the limits of any mindset you still have.

Your ideal is to operate daily through a mindless, thoughtless attitude.

Word replacement

WHEN YOU READ NAPOLEON Hill and Earl Nightingale again, you can see that they don't give the "mind" much credence. Practically, you can take any place where the words "mind", "subconscious", or "thought" are used and replace them with some word that doesn't require thoughts. They'll read the same if you can use the concept of an always-on inspiration instead.

Goal achievement can be super-charged when you don't use a mind or thoughts as part of your actions.

Consider words like conceive/conception, creative, vision, enjoy, envision. These don't involve the mechanical workings of a mind or tortured logic to "make sense". They instead have their roots in simple intuition and inspiration.

Let's take a couple of sentences from "The Science of Getting Rich" by Wallace D. Wattles:

There is a thinking stuff from which all things are made, and which permeates, penetrates, and fills the inter-spaces of the universe.

A thought in this substance produces the thing that is imaged by the thought.

Given that he wrote this material in a way that it could be readily understood by poorly-educated wage-earners of his day, you can see how the word "thought" has been widened into meaning almost anything.

Now, let's convert them over into something that is mind-less and thought-less:

There is an intuitive stuff from which all things are made, and which permeates, penetrates, and fills the inter-spaces of the universe.

A creative conception in this substance produces anything and everything that is imaged in that conception.

Always-on Inspiration

IT'S INTERESTING TO discover you are getting your ideas directly.

The mind becomes simply a limiting mechanism. It only slows your creative process down.

Mostly, the mind is full of negatives, and cautions. Any "problem", as noted by Byrne, is an invention of the mind.

When you take the inspired approach, every non-optimal situation has an opportunity to make things better.

This is your natural-state inspiration talking. And your inspiration and intuition become stronger as you trust them more.

Logic is useful in fewer and fewer applications. Argument and debate have no real use, as they were formulated by academics. They area all constructs of the mind, and mechanical.

Persuasion is creative. A model you can investigate for this is "Writing Non-Fiction" by Walter S. Campbell – his four-point process. And there is always Carnegie's "How to Win Friends and Influence People". Other books may be applicable, such as "Tested Sentences That Sell" by Elmer Wheeler.

You'll see that each of those books mentioned have thorough research behind them.

As you continue to release your thinking, the mind seems to have more and more holes in it. Longer spaces of just enjoying the world around you appear. No more amounts of words running through.

It's not that you don't fill the various functions that the mind did for you. But now you don't hold onto a mind to do them. So you can perceive and respond faster. You've just taken another layer away that has been slowing you down.

Which means more abilities will show up. Talents you've never known existed.

As for memories, I mentioned earlier that one theory holds that they've been placed in the body as "holographic" storage. So they will surface from time to time. And as you welcome them, all the negative thoughts you've had about them will drop away. As will any false assumptions and assignments about them. More than likely, your memory for the data you need will improve.

Your perception of Now will also change. You'll find that you are living in eternity already. There are several discussions of this in Byrne's "Greatest Secret" If you want to read various other teacher's observation about this. The short math of this is that: Yesterday is only memories, Tomorrow is only plans, Today in an ever-present moment.

Again, this is easier to experience than it is to describe. I'm just pointing out notes of my own observations in this area. And you are expected to test these for yourself.

Affirmations

NAPOLEON HILL'S USE of positive affirmations, based on Coue's work, is designed to raise a person up to a positive outlook and maintain that as a habit. By themselves, affirmations are useful when you get the positive feelings that go with them. They are criticized by those whose minds stop anything from working through their ingrained criticism of everything around them.

To maintain a constant always-on imagination and intuition, you will simply need to adopt "Welcoming" (releasing) as perpetual habit.

While Byrne describes this high state as happiness, the many uses of that term can throw you off. Also, people use different terms to describe what that state of "Zen" or "satori" bring to them as feelings.

Earl Nightingale described that optimal attitude as a calm, cheerful expectancy.

Napoleon Hill mentioned the need for a Positive Mental Attitude, and gave several lectures on that one point.

W. Clement Stone utilized a daily affirmation, "I feel healthy. I feel happy. I feel terrific!" as a means of calling that native state to the forefront of your attention. Then use that affirmation anytime your attitude drops or starts to sour.

Elsewhere, I've mentioned that a person will notice simplicity, enjoyment, peace, and abundance.

Once you've achieved this state, you'll have a baseline to compare any other types of feelings or even emotions that are running through your mind. Welcoming will then bring you back toward your own native baseline.

Sure, you can take that state higher.

The point is that whatever you are doing should forward your bliss. You don't have to be wildly enthusiastic or exhilarated all the time. But you can live in a constant "peace that passes understanding".

Just pick your terms that resonate with you. Because you'll know it when you feel it. And anything less than that just needs to be welcomed.

Action Steps

IN THIS BOOK, I'VE perhaps covered entirely too much material. But this is the point – to give you plenty of stuff so that you can choose and develop your own path to personal Freedom.

There is a bibliograpy attached, in addition to the books and resources I've mentioned above.

But I can't study them for you. This book is merely a stepping-off point.

Originally this book started off from a review of my "Go Thunk Yourself" self-help success book. I wanted to revisit what I had written ten years before and update all this material with what I've found since.

This updated version now comes eleven years after that.

While I've said it before, I have to apologize again for all the writing I've done. This book and those earlier ones were never really necessary. As you reach your high state for yourself, this is obvious.

All this book contains is just a very workable path that I created for myself, based on research that I found useful. And it's tailor-made for me – one size doe not fit all; your mileage will very definitely vary.

This final section of the book is to help you determine what guru's coaches, books, materials, or whatever it is that you may seem to want to help you with your own search, your own patch construction.

It's you who will have to be the final judge as to whether this book or any essay in it is workable or useful for your own personal improvement or development efforts. For at this writing, and as I've discovered these materials for myself, I've remained hard at work simply applying all this stuff – and it may or may not take a few more months or years or decades before I consider that my path is walked.

That time is just an arbitrary measure, though. And you'll soon see why if you don't already know.

This book, however, is supposed to be about you – and not about me. And if *you* were wanting a sequence of steps and sequences on what to do – how would a person approach this?

The key point I've uncovered overall is that Levenson's releasing technique is an undercut to every type of self-help philosophy and practice out there. It only makes whatever author you are reading work even better. Whatever you are doing, releasing as you go simply makes it all much better, more effective.

There are probably two approaches to this:

1. Skip around this book and read what gets your interest. Then apply this to your life and see it it help you improve your situation.
2. Study this in the sequence as presented, applying it as best you can while you go along, then revise your sequence of actions with the new material you find.

Either of these is correct – or even a combination of them. It's also perfectly OK to just put this book on a shelf for later, or just give it away to someone else.

If you haven't run into this already – every thing that you do is perfectly OK. It's your life, live it however you want.

The reason I wrote this was not to point out any particular character flaw or limitation you might have – quite the reverse. You are already a perfect being – and are already enlightened. This book is only a way of giving you data you may or may not have encountered or figured out for yourself. I just want to help you become even more perfect in living the life that you have in front of you.

One workable approach

1. Read through (or simply scan) the book and see what you want to come back to and study more thoroughly later. Make notes in the margin, add tabs, dog-ear the pages.
2. Make a short list of things you'd like to improve in your life. You can change this as much as you want later. You just want a record of where you were when you started.
3. Now, come back and set a certain time each day - in a place and time you won't be disturbed - to both study some more of this book and put it to use in your life. Work out activities which you can then prove to yourself whether what you just read was workable for you.
4. As you finish off the book, compare notes with where you are now and see if you've either acquired, achieved, or accomplished some of that list. Look to see if you are now more active, or if things are easier and more effortless now. Look at your own beingness and see if you have more certainty or better self-esteem.
5. Start over with your scheduled study and now work over how you can apply each and every datum of this book. This time, if you have questions about the material, get the books or look them up online so you can see the original materials this book was derived from. Most of them can be gotten for little cost, or the time you spend downloading these. But where you have the physical book to hand (or any other recorded version) you'll see that this is easier to study and cross-reference.
6. Once you get to the end of this third time through, check out your life at that point. Do you have more? Do you do more, are you still more active and effortless? How's your

self-confidence and love for those around you?

7. Then, review this book (and the additional references you've collected as part of this study) once a month or so to keep you on the track you set for yourself. You'll find that your understanding has improved, that you have many more lessons to learn in your life.

Daily Schedule

MANY PEOPLE HAVE FOUND that some simple structure in their lives helps to make the changes they want.

a) Get a certain place and time to do your studies. Some location you won't be disturbed.

b) Schedule out studying these materials – or other related materials of interest.

c) Listen or read inspirational or motivational materials every day. This can be at this time, or in addition – such as a daily commute to a job.

d) Work at maintaining a calm, even approach to life during your day. Nightingale had this as a "calm, cheerful expectancy". Levenson had this as courageousness, acceptance, and peace. Live from this level, and release anything that comes up which tries to knock you off this level. Welcome everything.

e) Get the new mental habit of releasing constantly. Anything that comes up – just let it go. Keep working at this until your mind is quiet, your inspirations are instantaneous, and your own world is at peace regardless of what happens in the world around you.

f) Then answer "What am I?" (if you haven't already...)

You'll see Freedom showing up around you in incredible amounts. Your Happiness, your Joy – all the Peace you could want is already within you. It's always been there. You've only needed some help to allow yourself to just let it out again.

What do you do after this? Anything you want. It will be an interesting, new way of living. One you haven't experienced in some time. I can't tell you what you are going to want to do at that point. No one else other than you can, actually. Because you are going to be a different person at that point. All the masks you have been wearing, all the different habituated responses which you considered "normal" have been gone for some time. What you'll see now is your own, native Self.

Believe it or not, there's even steps beyond that to take. But you'll know what to do at that point – and will need no book or recordings or videos to tell you what you have to do next.

And I wish you all the speedy progress you could want for yourself. For up ahead is something very new compared to how you've been treating yourself all this time.

It's not the Future. It's a better Now. The world around you is now *your* creation – just as you've been creating it all along.

The Key Data Behind Valid Self Help Books and Materials

OF ALL THE WORK I'VE done to date, this is perhaps the most important – and potentially the most damning.

None of this is an easy walk in the park. But it is vital that I tell you at this point.

There are a handful of metaphysical principles which all successful self help programs contain. I've already gone over a checklist to see if any particular self-help guru isn't delivering the goods. So now I hope to tell you what they do need to contain.

1. **"Thoughts create your reality."** See Huna principle 1, Earl Nightingale's "Strangest Secret", Napoleon Hill's "Think and Grow Rich", Haanel's "Master Key System", etc.
2. **"You can connect to a Higher Intelligence/the Universal to get answers and intuitive suggestions."** See Haanel, Hill (Chapter 14), most religions and philosophies cover this point. The Silva Method.
3. **"Self inspection and personal analysis is your real path – if you need one."** This is the key point to Buddhism, especially Zen. As well Jesus gave many examples of his own meditating in the wilderness. Lester Levenson's release technique.
4. **"Your persistence and faith determine your progress toward enlightenment."** See Hill's talks on "Burning Desire", and other New Thought authors' comments on concentration.

Now you will also see that they have a set of programmed steps to follow, but any system being sold or promoted right now have these, so that's a given. This separates real self-help from poetry or artwork or mere "inspirational quotes".

When you get down to the bottom-line basics, you'll see that the *real* push and drive is to get the individual up to the point where they can let their *own* abilities shine out and manifest. It is at that point where anything they could need or want simply shows up around them. All these other goals work are just the process of getting them confident in their own abilities so that they can and will – on their own.

These four points above are the common theory points which have to be present for any real self-help progress to be made. If they don't tell you these points pretty quickly, you don't have a path to follow – except to keep paying their salaries with your "donations."

But money is another trap and only useful as an introduction to the broader subject of self-actualization.

It's whether they actually tell you that self-actualization is possible which will tell you their intent. And then you will know everything about them.

OH, AND IF YOU FIND someone who isn't searching, who is completely calm and at peace with everything – and while meanwhile being quietly confident of themselves enough to be only interested in you and the people around them – realize you just met one of the real, rare, genuine articles. Treasure them and help them as you can. Don't try to keep up with the help you'll be getting from them, because they really and factually only exist to serve.

Those are the real deals. About one in ten million or more. Cherish them. And learn so you can "do greater things than these."

What Makes A Self Help Guru Really Successful?

UNFORTUNATELY, MOST of these guys and their marketing firms have this backward.

You only have to study my Scam-Free Book and the Preamble to Covey's 7 Habits to find out why:

Most guru's and "success coaches" are out there

to *sell benefits*.

They can and will give you a dozen solutions to any want or need you think you have. But Covey found in his study of a couple hundred years of success material in the U.S. – that the last 50 years were devoted to just attitude adjustment *instead of actually working out the underlying causation and eradicating it.*

Of course, I did my own study and completed most of it before I found Covey's work as a side-check on that research. I only took dead authors whose works were still being widely circulated, then looked for commonalities (crossovers) in them.

This wound up in my "Go Thunk Yourself" series.

But as I knew in follow-up research that something was missing. And only found that recently.

And in reviewing all this for my last book in this area then brought up the fact that I pull my own success from a wide-range of material – but only four main subject areas.

The point today is to cover how you can tell a real deal from a fake.

I mention (probably too much) that you need to be familiar with Maslow, Cialdini, and Levenson to know that you are scam[1]-free (see the book on this, as well as the scam-free checklist).

While a scammer and an honest practitioner can be separated by finding their actual intentions (but you still can't separate them from their money, different than the fools they ply) – even the people having great financial success in their marketing may not understand what they actually need to do to be the "real deal."

1. Real guru's aren't concerned with themselves as an example. The best will actually try not to bring their own successes up, since this then builds resistance by giving you a "hidden standard" to measure your own progress against.

2. Real guru's are interested more in your self-actualization than anything they say or do – or even in the materials they offer. ("...ye shall do even greater things than these...") They aren't just offering to help you cure physical ailments, get rich quick, have an incredible sex life, or "attract" that luxury car/huge house/expensive trinket you've "always" wanted?

3. There is no dogma or hyper-compartmented teachings to swallow wholesale. Real teachers will insist that you work this out for yourself and only accept something if and when you've proved it for yourself.

4. And while it's necessary to "make money" to survive in this culture, it's more to the point that people won't value something unless they have to contribute something first or as a result. Money, especially hard-earned income, is

---

1. http://robertworstell.com/books/get-your-self-scam-free/

one way to do this. CEO Space requires people to go out and learn by getting people to get investors contributing to their success.

And so this really gives you a four-point checklist to see if you have a fake or the real deal in front of you:

- Look up their website and see if it's personality and approval-driven. Does it have a lot of pictures of the principles with other celebrities?

- Do you have to buy extensive packages of materials which can only be used under certain conditions and agreements? Are you forbidden from improving on these materials or teaching your own version?

- Are these guru's and their staffs only really interested in how you are progressing with these materials? Do they give you a testimonial form to fill out? Or are they simply giving you solutions to insatiable desires – how rich is rich?

- Are you constantly being asked for more money every time you turn around. This can also be insidious, as they are putting pop-ups on their site to get you to sign up for their email course – then claiming they have XXX,XXX subscribers or "millions of satisfied customers worldwide!"

Now, take it as a given that since the vast majority of people on this planet are running on 95% subconscious habits, you are going to attract people into a real self-help study which can let them achieve enlightenment only by first telling them that "your lumbosis can be easily alleviated with high-powered and unique methods we have."

As well, that they can "live more abundant and prosperous lives" if they start doing such-and-so at such-and-such price per hour. Only when you tell them that *the reason they want all these things also has to be addressed* – that is the first time you are bringing up the point that self-actualization is the higher goal to *really* shoot for. Because only when they've had success in dealing with these relatively minor problems of having abundance or happiness or good health in their lives (which are actually native to everyone anyway) will they be able to see that there is something higher that they can and should be reaching for.

The final point – *do they deliver the goods*? Some certain fields of study have the problem of having promised their people that they can attain super-high personal states, but not having those actual courses and processes available for purchase at any prices. Zen Buddhism says at least that while many people have become bodhi/ achieved satori, others might take several lifetimes before they do – while some can get there in minutes, per Alan Watts. When you study up on a self-help guru, look to see if they are delivering a finite set of goods that is here right now.

If they are just selling you the "next great thing" with no end in site – realize you are their income source. And little else. Move on. Find yourself another guru, or become your own.

Hope this helps.

Personal Improvement Crossovers and Compartments

ALL LIFE, AT LEAST our humankind version of it, is severely compartmented. People live their lives in cloistered cubicles, even when they are right next to a person. Each of us lives very unique experiences – so much so that when a set of witnesses watch an accident happen, no two people have the same report.

And we keep our knowledge and our beliefs running in this same manner. Sciences are kept uniquely different in different fields. Medicine is even more refined – specialists for everything. Cancer treatment is by area of the body, not by type of cancer. (Even though all cancer has commonalities of causation and treatment.)

So we can take this to extremes, and live very individuated lives. It's even remarkable nowadays when people share the same thought simultaneously. Or have pets who "know" when you are sick or feeling down. People who are "empathetic" are valued highly.

But to study ancient philosophies and religious texts, our modern world is the anomaly. These books and scrolls and verbal traditions tell us that we are all connected. All interconnected. We can actually find out anything we want to whenever or wherever we choose.

Quantum Physicists have been some of the first scientists to discover this – that the presence of the operator causes the outcome of the experiment, no matter how well shielded. And so many of these have gone back to study philosophies, especially ancient Eastern texts, in order to understand what they had just ran into.

This is another indicator of scam or fraud – when they won't let you look at other data. Wide open studies like Huna tell you to use any part or all of what you find workable for yourself and improve on it or combine it with other studies. "Self-Help" corporations (with their own cult culture) will tell you not to "mix practices" and that studying related fields or authors is akin to the highest mortal sin possible.

Internet Coaching and Marketing guru's have this same problem. Once they train people to get out on the Internet for themselves, their consumers will find that they don't have all the answers and then leave – and might even demand their money back. (The most petulant of these can't stand to be blogged about, either.)

But the answers to any questions can be found simply when you look for crossovers from other fields.

The more I look for answers, the more I find. As long as you keep a truly open mind and are testing everything you find for workability, you find amazing material that can radically improve your life. You'll also find where studies and systems are missing huge chunks which would make them more workable.

My own results in looking for crossovers lead me to the four core studies which interacted as a "tetrad" and would result in real increase of personal ability, prosperity, and freedom: Huna, Silva Method, Levenson Release Technique, and New Thought bestsellers.

I invite you to study these four resources and find the crossovers for yourself – not just to accept what I say here.

And I can only tell you that by being truly open to the world around you, and seeing it for what it is – not what you think it should be or would like to change it into – only then will you see a remarkable world around you and be able to take advantage of the vast amount of opportunities ever present.

4 Goals To Achieve Which Will Save Your Life and Everyone Else as Well

I TEND TO LEARN FROM my "dreams", even when it's the one we share in living in this Universe.

And last night was a doozy. But what came from it is that when you release on goals in order to achieve them, you are actually helping everyone around you as well. So the bigger the goal, the more you help humankind in general.

Meaning, that if you really have concern for this planet and the people on it, you'll work on releasing the biggest goals you can dream of. We are all connected, after all.

These four goals (word them as you like):

- World Peace

- Abundance for every single person

- Balance in Nature, as we are part of it

- Personal Freedom for every single person

Now, I could tell you more about these (and have, in my various blog posts over the years), but the key point is that you need to deal with individuals to get this to work. Never, ever, the government. Because the government (like money) is a fiction, a contrivance and as you release more and more, it becomes obvious that people only use the concept of government to control, to gain approval, and to provide a false sense of security.

The next point it is that you never "fight" anything. That also doesn't work. You become the thing you are fighting. In order to dissolve a situation, you will need to simply welcome it and release it. Recognize it for what it is and let it go. It will then cease to have any effect on you. If you do need to do something, you'll get the intuitional inspiration of what to do. Don't "think" about it – just put it into motion.

As you start working on these broad goals to release, then you'll see how they interact, as well as other reasons you need to work on all four. Time permitting, I'll set these each up with the data I have and help you as possible with your own work.

4 studies to learn from

MY OWN BACKGROUND, was from some twenty years of following a corporate cult – although I've now examined and tested all that and found it all lacking. It was a great introduction to a wide world of philosophers, religious prophets, and spiritual guides, but it's a limited (as in dead-end) study.

When I started butting up against the limits of that subject, I started studying the core texts it was derived from. This lead to my "Go Thunk Yourself!" study, which lead me right into New Thought.

New Thought is a very wide umbrella which has incorporated a lot earlier philosophers, as well as the bulk of the really successful self-help books such as "Think and Grow Rich", "Science of Getting Rich", and "Master Key System."

Somewhere along those studies, I stumbled upon *Huna*. This is the oldest known surviving philosophy on this planet. And interestingly, owes its rebirth in popularity (at least in the Western world) to Max Freedom Long, who gave it it's name. (Practically, the subject was so immersed in the culture, that it didn't have a single name before that point, much like water has several names for its various forms.) Long was a New Thought student, but I found that out later.

The third study is *Silva Method*, after the work Jose Silva did in his life-long study of the human condition and how to improve it. This is very powerful stuff, more powerful than even its practitioners know. But in the last decade, they've seen how it's more broadly applicable than earlier known.

A fourth study is *Lester Levenson's release technique*. Also known as the Sedona Method. And there are other variants around – they all

work. Larry Crane and Hale Dwoskin, as well as Stephen Seretan –
all these have their own individual approaches, but they all trained
directly under Levenson and so got the real scoop on how to help
anyone achieve their own Freedom and Peace of Mind.

I use all four of these together as the most effective way to quickly
resolve personal situations and problems in my life.

Any of them individually would take you right on out to
enlightenment if you really, really studied and applied them. All
of them can also be toyed with to simply make your life more
comfortable.

My own use, with Haanel, Hill, and Wattles providing the
theoretical base – is to use the Alpha centering technique of Silva
to get into a high personal state in order to use Levenson's release
technique to simply let things go. Huna provides the glue to hold
everything together.

And I would tell you these four things:

1. Know we are all connected (7 principles of Huna).
2. Know how the universe works (New Thought authors as
    listed.)
3. Use Silva techniques to get into a personal high state of
    certainty.
4. Release with Levenson's techniques so that you drop the
    underlying desires which hold everything in place.

Where to get the data

I'VE WORKED TO REPUBLISH the key New Thought authors
through my LiveSensical site .

For Huna, I have Max Freedom Long's books there and also tell you to visit http://huna.org[2] , where you'll see all Serge Kahili King's work. Tad James' work is also recommended.

While Silva has undergone many transitions since Jose passed on, I'd still recommend getting a copy of his Ultra-Mind CD's as you can. These I know give you all the data you need to get going.

Levenson's original stuff is most easily found at Larry Crane's site. I've also found some original Levenson recordings on Hale's.

Practically, all of the above is also released to the Internet in various forms. So if you can afford to spend the time and bandwidth, you can get this all for "free."

The key point is to get this data, get your self proofed up and doing well, then tackle the bigger issues we all face as part of humankind.

---

2. http://huna.org/

An Apology for My Dreams and Yours

YOU SEE, THIS UNIVERSE we live in is almost exactly backwards from what we have been taught and have accepted as true. I, as you, have been pushing down this line, hoping for better answers as we go along.

And as I've covered at various points, both Levenson and Huna hold that the world around us is a dream, an illusion, "Maya". Joseph Campbell might call that statement a metaphor.

Anyone can start running into this as they start to work the top end of goals. While "having a nice car" or "having a loving relationship" are all very nice – you also have to recognize that you have also put "not having" as a goal much earlier than this and agreed to it as more powerful than anything else. Or you wouldn't have to now work at getting something to show up.

OK, back up: Levenson (and other ancient mystics and Masters) held that the being (meaning: "you" and "I") creates the world around them. This is, of course, the first principle in Huna – and covered in Napoleon Hill, Earl Nightingale, Charles Haanel, and a host of New Thought Authors. ("We become what we think about.")

Now, when you start working on goals, a lot of people (such as the example in Wattle's "Think and Grow Rich") work on getting *material things* to show up. This is also the basis of "The Secret" DVD, where people are being told how to "attract" things into their lives.

But the kicker is in the question, "Who is doing this attracting?" You then find out that the person is responsible for the Universe around them, that they put their own lack there first in order to solve it.

True.

Think it through for yourself.

It is not "you" and "the Universe". Haanel's whole "Master Key System" was a treatise on how you get up to the point that you figure out you put the whole thing there. Every religion and philosophy out there all were to help you internalize this one point: taking complete responsibility for having "mocked up" or created the exact problem you are dealing with.

And Canfield as well as Levenson (and Hubbard) make a point that you have to take responsibility for what you are doing and have done in order to do something about it.

Or, you can directly release the goal you created originally which was contrary to it, plus the desire below it.

This now explains why Levenson pointed out to get beyond having to have "stuff" and simply get your Freedom instead. Otherwise all manner of dire catastrophes ensue.

Why is this? You wreck your own game. What's the point of having everything you could possibly want – if you have worked all this long time to make sure you *didn't* have it to begin with?

All philosophies (not necessarily the religions based on them) contend that you are an infinite being in your own right. "There are no limits." as Huna covers.

But that same statement says we are all connected. And this explains the world around us as we see it. It appears to be composed of multiple versions of reality, all mushed together for our own group amusement. It is the game we are playing.

And you can cease playing this game at any point. The trick is to make sure that you don't have to keep playing any game at all – or you'll just put the whole thing back again. And so the problem that many of the rich had – where they would go bankrupt over and over and over – only to just regain their fortune each time.

But you have to know that the fiction of Money is just another game. So is the fiction of Government.

All around you, every single little and big thing – is all Maya – Illusion.

And you get rid of small parts of it by doing Goals Releasing. Literally, you sit on your Butt and release the reasons you don't have something and then it shows up. This is Stephen Seretan's KISS (Keep It Simple, Sweetheart) method he got directly from Levenson.

This stuff is too easy. Let's lay it out:

Use Silva Method to "go to Level" and meditate at Alpha or Theta (or Delta, if you can). Get this as a constant "on" condition – practice staying at this state during your whole day and night.

Release everything that shows up, taking these down to basic and sub-basic desires. After you've been releasing constantly for awhile and get fairly imperturbable, give yourself some big goals, such as: "I allow myself access to Infinite Intelligence." or "I allow myself Infinite Beingness." All this does is set the stage for some massive realizations about how this universe around you works – and how you put it there to begin with.

Keep on going "all the way out" and don't let up for *any* reason. Want your Freedom more than you want this Maya around you. You want to move from Mystic (initiate) to Adept (master) – which is only a single release away. (Which explains how Alan Watts quotes an artist who said that the attainment of real Zen [an ultimate satori state] could take some people lifetimes and others just minutes. See the Wikipedia article on Mysticism to see what's possible here.)

And there is no 4. Because once you get to that point, you really do see that you are only attracting your own lack – that there is nothing "out there" except what you put there, or not.

This is why all these guru's and coaches are so very amusing. Because while they are all helping you improve your success, they don't take it all the way out. They keep telling you how to "pimp your ride", or telling you how to drive more safely, or evade the cops – instead of letting you in on the secret of teleporting.

(That secret, by the way, is the same as telepathy: distance, all Space and Time, are fictions. We are *all* already intimately connected in the Now. Release on *that*.)

While there are "many paths up the mountain," you'll also quickly see that there never was a mountain to begin with.

But you knew that.

Coda

LET ME TELL YOU ABOUT another couple of interesting dreams I had.

We aren't concerned about the details of them, as much as the lesson I took away from having them.

(And this won't probably make much sense until you read it through a couple of times. Mostly because the theory is very basic to how this world around us is set up.)

I.

THE FIRST WAS ABOUT two forces found in this frame of reference around us, called Altos and Menos. But you could call them about anything.

Both are Love-based.

- Altos = Love + Thought

- Menos = Love + Physical Universe

Altos speeds up manifestation/attraction/demonstration of anything you really want or seems important.

Menos slows these down.

Love in both cases is the creation element. Create your thoughts, or create more physical universe.

The trick is that the physical universe (and this is held by several different sources) is just composed of condensed thought. The more people agree something exists, the solider and more "real" it gets.

So these two aren't actually equally opposed or balanced. By withdrawing Love from either side, the force in that equation is withdrawn.

The bottom line is in who decides how much Love or Thought to put there.

This is Be – or Self. Be is what causes Love to exist or function. Be creates all thought.

You can simply decide at any point to change your mind. That changes the world around you.

II.

THIS SECOND DREAM OCCURRED earlier last night. Again, it doesn't really matter about the details. It matters about the principle below it.

In the military, this describes an interesting phenomenon called "short-timer syndrome." People agreed to fill out a contract (in the volunteer military, not the draft) for a certain amount of time. The closer they got to getting out (finishing their contract), the more light-hearted and unmotivated they became. All they had to do was to "stay out of trouble" and they were done. So they'd do what they had to to "get by" – and very little else. Their uniforms were perfect, their area neat and clean.

But nothing would really get done. And since they knew all the rules, you really couldn't catch them at anything. You'd simply go get someone else to do it. Because there was no way to really threaten them with anything – they would just put up with you for another few months and then they'd be gone.

But you, on the other hand, had a long career in front of you. You can be sent on long tours of duties in foreign lands without recourse. So you toe the line.

No one was going to cut orders for a short-timer to go anywhere – they'd just have to cut another set of orders to bring them right back...

III.

ANYONE, AT ANY MOMENT can get this "short-timer syndrome." It just takes realizing that the physical universe has no hold on you whatsoever.

You just have to cross that thin line which separates Being from Doing and Having.

To do requires some sort of playing ground. And to have requires you accumulate stuff on that playing ground.

But real Be – not the approval-oriented fiction, but real certainty of Self and the unflappable peace that comes with it – this is the point. When you quit associating your Self with a body or any specific identity in this playing ground we call the Physical Universe, then you have achieved that rare state called satori or enlightenment or illumination.

And it's just that simple.

This is the point of Dr. Hew Len's modern Ho'o-pono-pono. This is the point to the Silva Method and Silva Ultramind. And even deeper, what Lester Levenson found when he discovered and developed the Sedona Method release technique.

For when you can't be controlled or need to control, when you don't need approval from anyone, when you are secure and safe regardless of the world around you (needing no physical situation in your life) – then and only then you have all the Freedom, Peace, and Joy you could ever want. And just slightly above that point: all the Peace of Mind you can handle and more.

All the self-help and personal development techniques will only take you so far. Right up to the brink, in fact.

But then you have to make the decision to step over that line.

Once you do, it's "all downhill" after that. Piece of cake. Easy rider stuff.

You'll find the personal meaning of "a peace that passes all understanding."

And resolving conflicts or troubles in this universe will become a detached hobby – if you want to go that route. When you get clear of all your own problems or wants or lacks (because you know you can create solutions any time you want) then it's moot whether you want to create and exert the energy necessary to do so.

Because you'll have all the Choice you could want after that point. You'll be at a permanent Zen state.

Now that doesn't mean you can't get all embroiled again in anything you choose. You created this world for yourself to begin with, after all. Just because you can be at that state all the time, doesn't mean you have to. It's a trade off.

But everyone should try it at least once in their lifetime.

The point is that it will be your conscious choice from that point forward.

IV.

FROM http://www.miraclesandinspiration.com/hooponopono3.html

Spirit, Superconscious, please locate the origin of my feelings, thoughts of (___________fill in the blank with your belief, feeling, thoughts__________).

Take each and every level, layer, area and aspect of my being to this origin. Analyze it and resolve it perfectly with God's truth.

Come through all generations of time and eternity. Healing every incident and its appendages based on the origin.

Please do it according to God's will until I am at the present.

Filled with light and truth, God's peace and love, forgiveness of myself for my incorrect perceptions.

Forgiveness of every person, place, circumstances and event which contributed to this, these feelings thoughts.

Basics of Releasing

THIS IS JUST A RECORD of the basics for you to refer to if you haven't done releasing before.

Actually, if you go to any of the various Levenson releasing technique sites, you'll find all the basics you could want. Additionally, you can get free downloads and materials, including CD's, which will cover this in far more detail and with examples.

The simplicity is just these two actions:

1. Accepting what is,
2. Letting it Go.

The ultimate goal is wanting Freedom more than you want the World. This will take you right on out to a high level of personal enlightenment.

As some had difficulty with this, the World was broken down into 4 singular "wantings" you use to relate with that World around you:

- Wanting Control

- Wanting Approval

- Wanting Security

- Wanting Separation/Oneness

The lower you go down the list, the deeper the level of the want.

The Wanting Control is often typified by frustration or impatience with people around us, as they simply aren't doing what we want them to do – or vice-versa. Like wanting a slow driver in front of you to speed up, for instance. Or talking to the TV and telling someone how they should change some behavior you noticed them doing.

Wanting Approval is a very common scene – popularity contests, or resentment at not being chosen for a team – any of these keep us stuck to behaviors where we are acting to please someone, or that we think others should get our OK before they do anything.

Wanting Security is far more basics. And needing to control or get approval is held in place by these. This unease is present with any time we are job hunting, or our position with a company or in life is threatened. Of course, this brings a lot more stress into our lives where we aren't in a peace-time activity. But it can also be the annoyance of a power outage, or bills you have to pay.

Wanting Separation or Oneness is ever present, but we are not usually aware of it. Wanting to be part of a group is of course a factor in wanting approval, but more basic. Wanting to "get away from it all" is the reverse – but is very basic. And might be the reason we have to have vacations at all. It's also the point of having people recognize your individuality.

There are definite feelings associated with all of these wants. As you start discovering these wants, you will see common feelings show up on certain ones. There may even be locations in the body where you have physical sensations when these feelings and wants occur.

Of course, use the below steps to release what you find as you find it. Practice will make this easier.

And remember – you can't do this wrong, you can't screw it up. No one is looking over your shoulder and giving you a grade on your performance. What happens when you release is only what happens for you. So be easy on yourself and do only what you can when you can. You'll make it eventually, regardless.

The six steps were revised from Levenson's own original series. But were changed only to make them more workable. Again, these are laid out in more detail through any of the various books and recordings you can find. Even videos online will explain these more.

The six steps are:

1. *You must want freedom more than you want approval, control, security, or separation/oneness.*
2. *Decide that you can release in the moment*
3. *Notice what you are feeling in the moment, and determine which of the four wants underlies that feeling, and then let the feeling go. (But don't hold onto a feeling if it's already gone in order to determine what want was present.)*
4. *Release constantly, regardless of what you are doing or who you are with.*
5. *If you feel "stuck", then simply let go of that stuck-feeling, or wanting to change that "stuckness."*
6. *Every time you release, you will probably feel lighter, happier, and freer. Often you need to release on any exhilaration you feel – so you can keep releasing.*

You can make a chart of the four needs and the six steps to keep in your wallet or purse or pocket – until you know them by heart and are able to release easily.

The idea is that you keep going with this line of practice until you can release instantaneously and near-automatically, any time you experience a negative or adverse feeling in your life.

Again, get the published material on this, or see some videos until these make perfect sense to you. You may even want to buy some of the intro materials or courses that these sites offer. Or attend seminars. What you do with this is up to you and what you want to achieve with your life.

Your Freedom Is.

Addenda

SOME OF THIS MATERIAL you may have covered before. Certainly Napoleon Hill's "Think and Grow Rich" is on almost everyone's bookshelf with dog-eared pages that contain underlined and highlighted lines.

I've collected the most salient excerpts for your quick introduction to other authors, all of which have something to do with the practical philosophy of goal achievement.

The Strangest Secret

An excerpt from How to Completely Change Your Life in 30 Seconds[1] by Robert C. Worstell, edited from notes on the talks of Earl Nightingale

Part I

I'D LIKE TO TELL YOU about the strangest secret in the world.

Some years ago, the late Nobel prize-winning Dr. Albert Schweitzer was asked by a reporter, "Doctor, what's wrong with men today?" The great doctor was silent a moment, and then he said, "Men simply don't think!"

It's about this that I want to talk with you. We live today in a golden age. This is an era that humanity has looked forward to, dreamed of, and worked toward for thousands of years. But since it's here, we pretty much take it for granted. We are particularly fortunate to live in the richest era that ever existed on the face of the earth ... a land of abundant opportunity for everyone.

But do you know what happens? Let's take 100 people who start even at the age of 25, do you have any idea what will happen to those men and women by the time they're 65? These 100 people believe they're going to be successful. If you would ask any of these if they wanted to be successful, you'd find out they did. They are eager toward life, there is a certain sparkle in their eye, an erectness to their carriage, and life seems like a pretty interesting adventure to them.

---

1. *http://livesensical.com/go/zon-cyl/*

But by the time they're 65, only one will be rich, four will be financially independent, five will still be working, and 54 will be broke.

Know what will happen to 100 individuals who start even at the age of 25, and who believe they will be successful? By the age of 65, only five out of 100 will make the grade! Why do so many fail? What happened to the sparkle that was there when they were 25? What became of the dreams, the hopes, the plans ... and why is there such a large disparity between what these people intended to do and what they actually accomplished?

When we say about 5 percent will achieve success, we have to define success and here is the best definition I've ever been able to find:

"Success is the progressive realization of a worthy ideal."

If a person is working toward a pre-determined goal and knows where they're going, that individual is a success. If they're not doing that, they're a failure. Success is the progressive realization of a worthy ideal.

Rollo May, the distinguished psychiatrist, wrote a wonderful book called "Man's Search for Himself", and in this book he says:

"The opposite of courage in our society is not cowardice... it is conformity."

And there you have the reason for so many failures. Conformity - people acting like everyone else, without knowing why or where they are going.

Now think of it, today we have millions of people age 65 and older. And most of them are broke. They're dependent on someone else for life's necessities.

We learn to read by the time we're seven. We learn to make a living by the time we're 30. Often by that time we're not only making a living, we're supporting a family. And yet by the time we're 65, we haven't learned how to become financially independent in the richest land that has ever been known.

Why? We conform! And the trouble is - most of us are acting like the wrong percentage group - the 95 who don't succeed.

And why do these people conform? Well, they really don't know. These people believe their lives are set by circumstances, by things that happen to them, by exterior forces. They're outer-directed people.

A survey was made one time of a lot of working individuals and they were asked, "Why do you work? Why do you get up in the morning?" 19 out of 20 had no idea. If you ask them, they'd tell you everyone gets up in the morning, and that's why they do it - because everyone else is doing it.

NOW LET'S GET BACK to our definition of success - who succeeds?

The only person who succeeds is the person who is progressively realizing a worthy ideal. It's the person who says, "I'm going to become this and then progressively works toward that goal.

A success is the school teacher who is teaching because that's what she wants to do. A success is the entrepreneur who starts his own company because that was his dream - that's what he wanted to do. A success is the sales person who wants to become the top-notch sales person in his company and sets forth on the pursuit of that goal.

A success is anyone who is doing deliberately a worthy predetermined job, because that's what he decided to do ... deliberately. But only one out of 20 does that! That's why today there really isn't any competition unless we make it for ourselves. Instead of competing, all we have to do is create.

You know, for 20 years I looked for the key which would tell you what would happen to a human being. Was there a key, I wanted to know, which would make the future a promise - something we could foretell to a large extent? Was there a key which would guarantee a person's becoming successful if they only knew about it - and knew how to use it?

Well there is such a key - and I've found it.

Have you ever wondered why so many people work so hard and honestly without ever achieving anything in particular, and why others don't seem to work hard, yet seem to get everything? They seem to have the "magic touch." You've heard people say, "Everything he touches turns to gold." Have you ever noticed that a person who becomes successful tends to continue to become more successful? And, on the other hand, have you noticed how someone who's a failure tends to continue to fail?

The difference is goals. Some of them have goals, some don't. People who have goals succeed because they know where they're going. It's that simple.

Think of a ship leaving a harbor, with the complete voyage mapped out and planned. The captain and crew know exactly where the ship is going and how long it will take - it has a definite goal. And 9,999 times out of 10,000, it will get there.

Now let's take another ship - just like the first - only let's not put a crew on it, or a captain at the helm.

Let's give it no aiming point, no goal, and no destination. We just start the engines and let it go. I think you'll agree that if it gets out of the harbor at all, it will either sink or wind up on some deserted beach - a derelict. It can't go anyplace because it has no destination and no guidance.

It's the same with a human being.

Take the salesman, for example. There's no other person today with the future of a good sales person. Selling today is the world's highest paid profession, if we're good at it and if we know where we're going. Every company needs top-notch sales people. And they reward their sales people - the sky's the limit for them. But how many can you find?

Someone once said, "The human race is fixed, not to prevent the strong from winning, but to prevent the weak from losing."

Any economy today can be likened to a convoy in time of war. The entire economy is slowed down to protect its weakest link, just as the naval convoy has to go at the speed that will permit its slowest vessel to remain in formation.

That's why it's so easy to make a living today. It takes no particular brains or talent to make a living and support a family today. We have a plateau of so-called "security", if that's what a person is looking for. We do, however, have to decide how *high* above this plateau we want to aim.

But let's get back to the "strangest secret" and the story I wanted to tell you today.

———————————

WHY DO PEOPLE WITH goals succeed in life and those without them fail?

Let me tell you something that, if you really understand it, will alter your life immediately. If you understand completely what I'm about to tell you, from this moment on - your life will never be the same again. You'll suddenly find that "good luck" is just attracted to you. The things you want just seem to fall in line, and from now on you won't have the problems, the worries, the gnawing lump of anxiety perhaps you've experienced before. Doubt, Fear, they'll be things of the past.

Here's the key to success - and the key to failure:

WE BECOME WHAT WE THINK ABOUT.

Throughout history, the great wise men and teachers, philosophers, and prophets have disagreed with one another on many different things. It is only on this one point that they are in complete and unanimous agreement.

Listen to what Marcus Aurelius, the great Roman Emperor, said: "A man's life is what his thoughts make of it."

Disraeli said this: "Everything comes if a man will only wait ... a human being with a settled purpose must accomplish it, and nothing can resist a will that will stake even existence for its fulfillment."

Ralph Waldo Emerson said this: "A man is what he thinks about, all day long."

William James said: "The greatest discovery of my generation is that human beings can alter their lives by altering their attitudes of mind. We need only in cold blood act as if the thing in question were real, and it will become infallibly real by growing into such a connection with our life that it will become real. It will become so knit with habit and emotion that our interests in it will be those which characterize belief." He also said, "If you only care enough for a result, you will almost certainly attain it. If you wish to be rich, you will be rich. If you wish to be learned, you will be learned. If you wish to be good, you will be good - only you must, then, really wish these things, and wish them exclusively, and not wish at the same time a hundred other incompatible things just as strongly."

In the Bible, you read in Mark 9:23, "If thou cans't believe, all things are possible to him that believeth."

My old friend Dr. Norman Vincent Peale put it this way: "This is one of the greatest laws in the universe. Fervently do I wish I'd discovered it as a very young man. It dawned on me much later in life and I found it to be my greatest discovery outside of my relationship with God. The great law briefly and simply stated is: If you think in negative terms, you will get negative results. If you think in positive terms, you will achieve positive results."

"That is the simple fact", he went on to say, "which is the basis of an astonishing law of prosperity and success. In three words: Believe and Succeed."

William Shakespeare put it this way, "Our doubts are traitors and make us lose the good we oft might win by fearing to attempt."

George Bernard Shaw said: "People are always blaming their circumstances for what they are. I don't believe in circumstances. The people who get on in this world are the people who get up and look for the circumstances they want, and if they can't find them, make them."

Well, it's pretty apparent, isn't it? And every person who discovered it believed, for a while, that he was the first one to work it out.

We become what we think about.

Now it stands to reason that a person who is thinking about a concrete and worthwhile goal is going to reach it, because that's what he's thinking about - and we become what we think about. Conversely, the person who has no goal, who doesn't know where he's going, and whose thoughts must therefore be thoughts of confusion, anxiety, fear, and worry will become what he thinks about. His life becomes one of frustration, fear, anxiety and worry. And if he thinks about nothing ... he becomes nothing.

HOW DOES IT WORK? WHY do we become what we think about? Well, I'll tell you how it works - as far as we know - but to do this I want to tell you about a situation that parallels the human mind.

Suppose a farmer has some land - and it's good, fertile land. The land gives the farmer a choice. He may plant in that land whatever he chooses. The land doesn't care what is planted. It's up to the farmer to make the decision.

Remember, we are comparing the human mind to the land, because the mind, like the land, doesn't care what you plant. It will return what you plant, but it doesn't care what you plant.

If the farmer plants two seeds - one a seed of corn, the other nightshade, a deadly poison. He digs two little holes in the land, plants both seeds - one corn, the other nightshade. He covers up the holes, waters, and takes care of the land, what will happen?

Invariably, the land will return what's planted. So up come the two plants - one corn, one poison. As it's written in the Bible, "As ye sow, so shall ye reap." Remember, the land doesn't care. It will return poison in just as wonderful abundance as it will corn. So up come the two plants - one corn, the other poison.

The human mind is far more fertile, far more incredible and mysterious than the land, but it works the same way. It doesn't care what we plant ... success ... or failure. A concrete, worthwhile goal ... or confusion, misunderstanding, fear, anxiety, and so on. But what we plant it must return to us.

You see, the human mind is the last, great unexplored continent on Earth. It contains riches beyond our wildest dreams. It will return anything we want to plant. You might say, "Well if that's true, why don't people use their minds more?"

I think they've figured out an answer to that one, too. Our mind comes as standard equipment at birth. It's free. And things that are given to us for nothing, we place little value on.

Things that we pay money for, we value.

The paradox is that exactly the reverse is true. Everything that's really worthwhile in life came to us free - our minds, our souls, our bodies, our hopes, our dreams, our ambitions, our intelligence, our love of family and children and friends and country. All these priceless possessions are free.

But the things that cost us money are actually very cheap and can be replaced at any time. A good man can be completely wiped out and make another fortune. He can do that several times. Even if our home burns down, we can rebuild it. But the things we got for nothing - we can never replace.

The human mind isn't used because we take it for granted. Familiarity breeds contempt. Our mind can do any kind of job we assign to it, but generally speaking, we use it for little jobs instead of big ones.

Universities have proved that most of us are operating on 10 percent or less of our abilities.

––––––

SO DECIDE NOW. WHAT is it you want? Plant your goal in your mind. It's the most important decision you'll ever make in your entire life.

What is it that you want? Do you want to be an outstanding sales person, an outstanding worker at your particular job? Do you want to go places in your company ... in your community? Do you want to get rich? All you have got to do is plant that seed in your mind, care for it, work steadily toward your goal, and it will become a reality.

It not only will, there's no way that it cannot. You see, that's a law - like the laws of Sir Isaac Newton, the laws of gravity. If you get on top of a building and jump off, you'll always go down - you'll never go up.

And it's the same with all the other laws of nature. They always work. They're inflexible.

Think about your goal in a relaxed, positive way. Picture yourself in your mind's eye as having already achieved this goal. See yourself doing the things you will be doing when you have reached your goal.

Ours has been called the "phenol-barbitol age", the age of ulcers and nervous breakdowns and tranquilizers. At a time where medical research has raised us to a new plateau of good health and longevity, far too many of us worry ourselves into an early grave - trying to cope with things in our own little personal ways, without learning a few great laws which would take care of everything for us.

These things we bring on ourselves, through our own habitual ways of thinking.

Everyone of us is the sum total of our own thoughts. We are where we are because that's exactly where we really want to be - whether we'll admit that or not. Each of us must live off the fruit of our thoughts in the future, because what you think today and tomorrow - next month and next year - will mold your life and determine your future.

YOU'RE GUIDED BY YOUR MIND.

I remember one time I was driving through eastern Arizona and I saw one of those giant earth moving machines roaring along the road with what looked like 30 tons of dirt in it - a tremendous, incredible machine - and there was a little man perched way up on top with the wheel in his hands, guiding it. As I drove along I was struck by the similarity of that machine to the human mind.

Just suppose you're sitting at the controls of such a vast source of energy. Are you going to sit back and fold your arms and let it run itself into a ditch? Or are you going to keep both hands firmly on the wheel and control and direct this power to a specific, worthwhile purpose? It's up to you. You're in the driver's seat.

You see, the very law that gives us success is a double-edged sword. We must control our thinking. The same rule that can lead people to lives of success, wealth, happiness, and all the things they ever dreamed of - that very same law can lead them into the gutter. It's all in how they use it ... for good or for bad.

This is the "Strangest Secret" in the world! Now, why do I say it's strange, and why do I call it a secret? Actually, it isn't a secret at all. It was first promulgated by some of the earliest wise men, and it appears again and again throughout the Bible. But very few people who have learned it understand it. That's why it's strange, and why for some equally strange reason it virtually remains a secret.

I believe that you could go out and walk down the main street of your town, and ask one person after another what the secret of success is - and you wouldn't run into one person in a month who could tell you.

Now this information is enormously valuable to us - if we really understand it and apply it. It's valuable to us not only for our own lives, but the lives of those around us - our family, employees, associates, and friends.

Life should be an exciting adventure - it should never be a bore. Everyone should live fully, be alive, they should be glad to get out of bed in the morning. They should be doing jobs they like to do because they do them well.

One time I heard Grove Patterson - the great, late editor of the Toledo Daily Blade - make a speech. As he concluded his speech he said something I've never forgotten: "My years in the newspaper business have convinced me of several things. Among them, that people are basically good. And that we came from some place - and we're going some place. So we should make our time here an exciting adventure. The Architect of the Universe didn't build a stairway leading nowhere."

And the greatest teacher of them all, the carpenter from the plains of Galilee, gave us the Secret time and time again,

"As ye believe, so shall it be done, unto you."

Part II

IN THE FIRST PART OF this talk, I explained the Strangest Secret in the world, and how it works.

Now I want to explain how you can prove to yourself the enormous returns possible in your own life by putting the secret to a practical test. I want you to make a test that will last 30 days. It isn't going to be easy, but if you give it a good try, it will completely change your life, for the better.

Back in the 17th century, Sir Isaac Newton - the English mathematician and natural philosopher - gave us the natural laws of physics, which apply as much to human beings as they do to the movement of bodies in the universe. One of these laws is that, "For every action, there is an equal and opposite reaction." Simply stated, as it applies to you and me, is that we can achieve nothing unless we pay the price.

The results of your 30 day experiment will be in the exact proportion to the effort you put forth. To be a doctor, you must pay the price of long years of difficult study. To be successful in selling - and remember that each of us succeeds to the extent of our ability to sell: selling our families on our ideas, selling education in schools, selling our children on the advantages of living a good and honest life, selling our associates and employees on the importance of being exceptional people - to, of course, the profession of selling itself. But to be successful in selling our way to the good life, we must be willing to pay the price.

Now what is that price? Well, it's many things:

First, it's understanding emotionally as well as intellectually, we literally become what we think about. We must control our thoughts if we are to control our lives. It's understanding fully that, "As ye sow, so shall ye reap."

Second, it's cutting all fetters away from the mind, and permitting it to soar as it was divinely designed to do. It's the realization that your limitations are self-imposed - and that the opportunities today are enormous beyond belief. It's rising above narrow-minded pettiness and prejudice.

Third, it's using all your courage to force yourself to think positively on your own problem - to set a definite and clearly-defined goal for yourself, to let your marvelous mind think about your goal from all possible angles, to let your imagination speculate freely upon many possible solutions, to refuse to believe there are any circumstances sufficiently strong to defeat you in the accomplishment of your purpose, to act promptly and decisively when your course is clear, and to keep constantly aware of the fact that right now you are at this moment standing in the middle of your own acres of diamonds as Russell Conwell used to point out.

Fourth, save at least 10 percent of every dollar you earn.

It's also remembering that no matter what's your present job, it has enormous possibilities - if you're willing to pay the price.

Let's go over the important points and the price each of us must pay in order to achieve the wonderful life that can be ours. It is, of course, worth any price.

1. You will become what you think about.

2. Remember the word "Imagination" and let your mind begin to soar.

3. Courage - concentrate on your goal every day.

4. Save ten percent of what you earn, and

5. Action - ideas are worthless unless we act on them.

———

I'LL TRY TO OUTLINE the 30 day test I'd like you to make. Keep in mind that you have nothing to lose in making this test and everything you could possibly want to gain.

There are two things that could be said of everyone: each of us wants something, and each of us is afraid of something.

I want you to write on a card what it is you want more than anything else. It may be more money. Perhaps you'd like to double your income or make a specific amount of money. It may be a beautiful home. It may be success at your job. It may be a particular position in life. It could be a more harmonious family. Each of us wants something.

Write down on your card specifically what it is you want. Make sure it's a single goal and clearly defined. You needn't show it to anyone, but carry it with you so that you can look at it several times a day. Think about it in a cheerful, relaxed, positive way each morning when you get up, and immediately you have something to work for - something to get out of bed for, something to live for.

Look at it every chance you get during the day and just before going to bed at night. As you look at it, remember that you must become what you think about, and since you're thinking about your goal, you realize that soon it will be yours. In fact, it's really yours the moment you write it down and begin to think about it.

Look at the abundance all around you as you go about your daily business. You have as much right to this abundance as any living creature. It's yours for the asking.

Now we come to the difficult part. Difficult because it means the formation of what is probably a brand-new habit, and habits are not easily formed: Stop thinking about what it is you fear. Each time a fearful or negative thought comes into your mind, replace it with a mental picture of your positive and worthwhile goal. And there will come times when you'll feel like giving up. It's easier for a human being to think negatively than positively.

That's why only five percent are successful! You must begin now to place yourself in that group.

For 30 days, you must take control of your mind. It will think about only what you permit it to think about. Each day for this thirty-day test, do more than you have to do. In addition to maintaining a cheerful, positive outlook - give more of yourself than you've ever done before. Do this, knowing that your returns in life must be in direct proportion to what you give. The moment you decide on a goal to work for, you are immediately a successful person.

You are then in that rare and successful category of people who know where they are going. Out of every hundred people, you belong to the top five. Don't concern yourself too much with HOW you're going to achieve your goal - leave that completely to a power greater than yourself. All you have to know is WHERE you're going. The answers will come to you of your their own accord, and at the right time.

Remember these words from the Sermon on the Mount - and remember them well. Keep them constantly before you this month of your test:

> *"Ask, and it shall be given you. Seek, and ye shall find.*
>
> *Knock, and it shall be opened unto you.*

For every one that asketh, receiveth.

And he that seeketh, findeth.

And to him that knocketh, it shall be opened."

It's as marvelous and as simple as that. In fact, it's so simple that in our seemingly complicated world, it's difficult for an adult to understand that all he needs is a purpose and faith.

FOR 30 DAYS, DO YOUR very best. Go at it as you've never done before. Not in a hectic fashion - but with a calm, cheerful assurance that time well spent will give you the abundance and return you deserve and want. Devote your thirty-day test to completely giving of yourself without thinking of giving anything in return - and you'll be amazed at the difference it makes in your life. No matter what your job, do it as you've never done it before - for 30 days. And if you've kept your goal before you every day, you'll wonder and marvel at this new life you've found.

Dorothea Brande, the outstanding editor and writer discovered it for herself and tells about it in her fine book, "Wake Up and Live". Her entire philosophy is reduced to the words: "*Act as if it were impossible to fail.*" She made her own test, with sincerity and faith - and her entire life was changed to one of overwhelming success.

You make your test - for 30 full days. Don't start your test until you've made up your mind to stick with it. You see, by being persistent, you're demonstrating faith. Persistence is just another word for faith. If you didn't have faith, you'd never persist. If you should fail in your first 30 days, by that I mean if you should suddenly find yourself overwhelmed by negative thoughts, you've got to start over again from that point and go thirty more days.

Gradually, your new habit will form. Until you find yourself one of the wonderful minority to whom nothing is impossible.

And don't forget the card - it's vitally important to this new way of living. On one side of the card, write your goal, whatever it may be. On the other side, write the words we've quoted from the Sermon on the Mount: "Ask, and it shall be given you. Seek, and ye shall find. Knock, and it shall be opened unto you."

In your spare time during your test period, read books that will help you - inspirational books like the Bible, Dorothea Brande's "Wake Up and Live", "The Magic of Believing" by Claude Bristol, "Think and Grow Rich" by Napoleon Hill, and other books that instruct and inspire.

Nothing great was ever accomplished without inspiration. See that during these crucial first thirty days, your own inspiration is kept at a peak. And above all, don't worry. Worry brings fear, and fear is crippling. The only thing that could cause worry during this test is trying to do it all yourself. Know that all you have to do is to hold your goal before you. Everything else will take care of itself. Remember also to keep calm and cheerful. Don't let petty things annoy you and get you off course.

Since making this test is difficult, some will say, "Why should I bother?" Look at the alternative: No one wants to be a failure, no one really wants to be a mediocre individual, no one wants a life that is constantly filled with fear, and worry, and frustration. Therefore, remember that you must reap that which you sow. If you sow negative thoughts, your life will be filled with negative things. If you sow positive thoughts - your life will be cheerful, positive, and successful.

NOW, GRADUALLY, YOU will tend to forget what you have heard on this recording. Keep reminding yourself of what you must do to form this new habit. Gather your whole family around at regular intervals and listen to what's been said here.

Most people will tell you that they want to make money, without understanding this law. The only people who make money work in a mint.

The rest of us must earn money. This is what causes those who keep looking for something for nothing, or a free ride, to fail in life. The only way to earn money is in providing people with services and products which are needed and useful. We exchange our time and our product or service for the others' money. Therefore the law is that our financial return will be in direct proportion to our service.

Success is not the result of making money; making money is the result of success - and success is in direct proportion to our service.

Most people have this law backwards. They believe you're successful if you make a lot of money. The truth is that you can only earn money after you're successful.

It's like the man who stands in front of the stove and says to it: "Give me heat and then I'll add the wood."

How many men and women do you know, or do you suppose there are today, who take the same attitude toward life? There are millions.

We've got to put the fuel in before we can expect heat. Likewise, we've got to be of service first before we can expect money. Don't concern yourself with the money. Be of service ... build ... work ... dream ... create! Do this and you'll find there is no limit to the prosperity and abundance that will come to you.

Prosperity is built on a law of mutual exchange. Any person who contributes to prosperity, must prosper in turn himself. Sometimes the return will not come from those you serve. But the return must come to you from some place. Because that's the law: For every action, there is an equal and opposite reaction.

As you go daily in your 30-day test period, remember that your success will always be measured by the quantity and quality of the service you render. And money is a yardstick for measuring this service. No man can get rich himself unless he enriches others.

Now there are no exceptions to this law. You can drive down every street and from your car estimate the service that is being rendered by the people living on that street. Had you ever thought of this yardstick before? It's interesting. Some, like ministers or priests or other devoted people, measure their returns in the realm of the spiritual - but again, their returns are equal to their service.

Once this law is understood, any thinking person can tell his own fortune. If he wants more, he must be of more service to those from whom he receives his return. If he wants less, he has only to reduce his service.

This is the price you must pay for what you want. If you believe you can enrich yourself by deluding others, you can only end by deluding yourself. It may take some time, but as surely as you breathe, you'll get back what you put out. Don't ever make the mistake of thinking you can avert this. It's impossible. The prisons and the streets where the lonely walk are filled with people who tried to make new laws just for themselves. We may avoid the laws of man for a while, but there are greater laws that cannot be broken.

AN OUTSTANDING MEDICAL doctor recently pointed out six steps that will help you realize success:

1. Give yourself a definite goal.

2. Quit running yourself down.

3. Stop thinking of all the reasons you cannot be successful and instead, think of all the reasons why you can.

4. Trace your attitudes back through your childhood and try to discover where you first got the idea you couldn't be successful - if that's the way you've been thinking.

5. Change the image you have of yourself by writing out the description of the person you'd like to be.

6. Act the part of the successful person you have decided to become.

The doctor who wrote those words is the noted West Coast psychiatrist, Dr. David Harold Fink.

Do what the experts since the dawn of recorded history have told you you must do. Pay the price - by becoming the person you've wanted to become. It's not nearly as difficult as it is living unsuccessfully.

Make your 30-day test, then repeat it... then repeat it again. Each time it will become more a part of you until you'll wonder how you could have ever have lived any other way.

Live this new way and the flood-gates of abundance will open and pour over you more riches than you may have dreamed existed. Money? Yes, lots of it.

But what's more important, you'll have peace ... you'll be in that wonderful minority who lead calm, cheerful, successful lives.

Start today. You have nothing to lose - but you have your whole life to win.

Napoleon Hill – Fuel A Burning Desire

NAPOLEON HILL MET AN interesting person on one of his very first assignments as a reporter for a small country newspaper. And what was supposed to be an hour-long interview stretched out three days. At the end of this, he accepted a non-paid commission which lasted 20 years and affected him the rest of his life – giving him continuing successes.

Andrew Carnegie was one of his first interview subjects. Carnegie had an odd request. He saw something in Hill that could make it possible. Carnegie's commission: to interview a given set of famous and successful person and, from these varied life experiences, collect and distill a single practical success philosophy anyone could apply to improve their own quality of life.

Carnegie knew there was a common theme present, as he'd seen it with his own eyes when he climbed from the steel-workshop floor up to owner. And also knew that the government-run schools weren't training it - as he hired people with little formal education, who then became leaders of men and millionaires in their own right.

For Hill, this was an incredible opportunity. Hill had been born in a one-room log cabin in southwest Virginia. And tells in his books about the various tough times his family had on a dirt-poor farm. He had made it through school and got onto a backwoods newspaper as a cub reporter, looking for a big break – and this could be it.

However, Carnegie only offered to reimburse him for out-of-pocket expenses – and he was to interview over 500 of the most famous people of that time to distill their own success principles. But the rest is history.

Almost exactly 20 years after that Carnegie interview, Hill reached the point of distilling these interviews into a single philosophy in 1928. While he published this in a home-study course titled "The Law of Success", his real personal success was when he set about to solve the main problem the "Great Depression" had – and why he felt it was continuing. And from this 12-volume set, he distilled a single book that could be easily understood by the man on the street with just an average education. Titled "Think and Grow Rich", this went on to become perhaps the best selling self-help book in America.

In this book, Hill wrote about how to essentially recession-proof your life. He gave a simple way to always wind up a financial and material success if you just know and follow these few principles.

Hill had 13 points to his masterpiece which went far beyond just becoming rich or prosperous

In short:

1. Develop a burning desire to achieve in your life.
2. Develop your faith in yourself.
3. Use auto-suggestion to reprogram your mind.
4. Obtain the specialized knowledge you need.
5. Strengthen your creative imagination.
6. Utilize organized planning toward your goal.
7. Reach decisions promptly - and stick to them..
8. Develop and practice persistence.
9. Develop a Master Mind group of associates.
10. Recognize Love as a driving force.
11. Utilize your subconscious mind
12. Use your brain as an antenna for broadcasting and receiving inspiration.

13. Welcome Sixth Sense input.

Think and Grow Rich continued his research from his earlier master-work, "Law of Success".

Hill wanted to help the world throw off the remaining vestiges of the Great Depression. What he did was to create a handbook which went far beyond merely amassing money, but became a modern classic which probably one out of every three people has read or knows someone who has read this book and uses its data.

We can boil that bestseller down to even simpler core principles which repeat through his book - so we can then use those to re-build our own life into what we've always wanted.

The key point is concentrating on the core desire or life-purpose you want to achieve.

This is the idea behind Hill's BURNING DESIRE. And Dale Carnegie also put this in the front of his book - in the sections on how to get the most out of it.

> *"If you wish to get the most out of this book, there is one indispensable requirement, one essential infinitely more important than any rule or technique. Unless you have this one fundamental requisite, a thousand rules on how to study will avail little, And if you do have this cardinal endowment, then you can achieve wonders without reading any suggestions for getting the most out of a book.*
>
> *"What is this magic requirement? Just this: a deep, driving desire to learn, a vigorous determination to increase your ability to deal with people.*

"How can you develop such an urge? By constantly reminding yourself how important these principles are to you."

If you look closely in those few paragraphs, you'll see the same principles at work that Hill tells about.

A deep, driving desire - developed by constantly reminding yourself.

Hill suggested 6 steps to formulating this burning desire. While his approach in this book was to remedy the widespread fear of lack, it will do for any goal:

1. Fix in your mind the exact amount of money you desire.
2. Determine what you intend to give in return.
3. Establish a definite date when you intend to possess that sum.
4. Create a definite plan and begin at once.
5. Write out a clear, concise statement of the amount, it's date certain to have it, what you intend to give in return, and describe your plan clearly.
6. Read your written statement aloud, twice daily (evening before bed and very first thing in the morning - and feel yourself already in possession of the money.

It's really that simple - and millions have put this sequence or some variation to work in their own lives with incredible success.

There are reasons this works.

A. *Any lack of accomplishing anything is simply due to dispersal instead of concentration.* Once you concentrate everything you have, all your abilities, into a single channel of attention, then you will eliminate or handle every single obstacle that comes in between you and your goal. The key word is concentration.

B. *You have to give before you can get.* Nothing appears out of the blue, exactly. You'll find people had already been giving far more than they had to. They spent extra time and attention on the job at hand to make sure that it was of far more value than was requested. So their employer got more than was paid for. Anything they sold was far better quality and a lower price than it was obviously worth - a true bargain.

C. *Plan your work, work your plan.* If the plan doesn't work, then revise and start it again - immediately. That's the key. Get started right now on what you should be doing. Don't think it over any further. Strike while the iron is hot. And stick to that plan until you run into something unworkable, or something you hadn't foreseen - then rework the plan and go hammer-and-tongs at it again. Immediately.

D. *Remind yourself daily* of exactly where you are going, what you are giving, what you are doing, and realize it's already there and already yours - that all your steps are just making it arrive faster. You have to develop a calm knowing that all you really want is already there. That's the reason for the note and reading it daily.

And we can then add additional steps, which are less approved by our common society, but are incredibly more effective than anything we've ever tried to learn in schools:

E. *Connect with the Infinite daily.* Practice your intuition skills and they will improve. Don't rely on your thinking to carry you through, but be willing to look beyond your analytical thoughts right through to your creative core - and tap into this endless source for your own brilliant flashes of solution.

F. *Realize that the love you feel and share for those around you is key to your connection to the Infinite* - it serves as motivation and reward. As you develop this appreciation, it will grow. And all those you work with will be able to share in this - their own intuitive skills will bring you new data and approaches which you can all share toward your common goals. Creative imagination runs on love, which is the most vital and primal force in this universe - and which is responsible for creating all you see around you.

G. *Work with what you know and never second-guess it.* While we'll deal with this later, the key point now is to follow Hill's suggestion and just make your decisions quickly and stick to it. Your first idea is more often than not your best idea. Get it done. Once you teach yourself this discipline, it simplifies your life - things speed up as you get more efficient.

H. *Join, build, and form an association of like-minded individuals.* Both immediately around you in terms of associates at your work-place, and also meetings you can attend at remote locations annually or more frequently. This would also include people you might meet online and can only converse with through that medium. Such an association will reinforce your common goals and gain far more together than the individual parts of it could. This is Hill's Master Mind.

NOW, OF COURSE, I COULD sit and write chapters on each point above - but that's what Hill did, after all. Where you study and restudy Hill's master-work ("Think and Grow Rich" or "Law of Success"), you'll come to a greater understanding and use of his data. If you only studied and internalized Hill's works alone, anything you wanted would already be yours.

Serge Kahili King – Live Lessons from Long Ago

SERGE KAHILI KING'S training began with his father, who was assigned by the British Diplomatic Corps to Hawaii in 1911. Owing to a unique mystical experience, the elder King met and was adopted by an Hawaiian family. They trained King's father in an ancient tradition of Hawaiian shamanism.

At 14, Serge began his training under his father in these ways, but his father died within 3 years of his starting. Fortunately, Serge was adopted by the Kahili family as a grandson. He started traditional education with his uncle which continued for many years, interspersed with college degrees (a Bachelor's in Asiatic Studies in Colorado, a Master's in International Management in Arizona, and a Doctorate of Psychology in California). Interspersed with this formal Western training was spending 7 years studying under an West African shaman while also participating in humanitarian programs as part of the Catholic Relief Services.

King's uncle continued working with his nephew until, as Serge tells it, "... I was training with my uncle at that time and finally decided that this knowledge, based on what I had learned from them, based on Africa, and based on what I knew of the world situation, this knowledge was too precious not to share." The result of this was the organization Aloha International, which has as its purpose the dissemination of Hawaiian traditions and the wide knowledge Dr. King has accumulated.

Since the point where he realized that all the truth he needed to know was already his for the asking, he has been working to help other people find that truth which lies within themselves.

It is just our fortune that he is also an accomplished writer and speaker, having produced more books, videos, seminars, recordings, and other published works on the subject of Huna than any other known author in history.

I bring this short lecture to you to tell you of the incredible historic basis of these principles you are studying – and as well to brief you on the 7 basic principles which explain not only how this Universe works – but as well as that 12-volume "Law of Success" which Hill authored.

These 7 principles also explain how immutable Laws like the Golden Rule and the Law of Attraction work.

Again, like any of these authors – you could study King and Huna for the rest of this life and use that as a path almost solely to regain your own Freedom, Happiness, and Joy from here on out. So open your heart to understand these truths as you set your mind aside.

THE HUNA PRINCIPLES

Serge Kahili King speaking from Kauai

ALOHA! GREETINGS TO you, and to this ocean and to this land, to this wind and to this sky! I want to share with you a part of the Hawaiian cultural heritage.

A very long time ago in the islands of the Pacific, there were wise men and women who looked at the world, who observed the patterns of nature, the behavior of animals and plants, human beings, and they came to some conclusions about life, about what life is all about, about how life works. And they gave a name to this knowledge. They called it Huna, Ka Huna, the secret, the inner knowledge, the hidden knowledge.

And from this knowledge they developed seven ideas, seven principles, and these are what I want to share with you. The people who did this, who practiced this knowledge, were called Kapua; nowadays we might call them Shaman. And they had a very special way of looking at life, of seeing.

1. **IKE** - our ideas create our reality.

2. **KALA** - there are no limits.

3. **MAKIA** - energy flows where attention goes.

4. **MANAWA** - now is the moment of power.

5. **ALOHA** - to love is to be happy with.

6. **MANA** - all power comes from within.

7. **PONO** - effectiveness is the measure of truth.

Now the first of these ideas in Hawaiian is called **IKE** (ee-kay). And the idea in English is **The world is what you think it is**. This life of ours is a dream, our dream, a dream that we share with other people, that we share with the earth; a dream that we also share with ourselves alone. It's a way of saying that this dream of our experience, this reality as we call it, comes from inside, comes from our thoughts, our ideas, our beliefs, our fears, our desires, our angers and our pleasures. That all of the ways that we think produces this experience of ours. That from night comes day, from thought comes reality.

If we would change this reality, says this knowledge, this philosophy if you will, if we would change this reality, then we must change ourselves. And it is wasted energy to try to change the outer world alone, but if we would truly change the outer world we must go within and find that place within us which is creating the outer world, and change that. Change that idea, change that fear to hope, change that anger to love, change that belief in lack to a belief in abundance. This is IKE, working from within to create the outer.

This is the most important of the ideas, and all of these ideas that we're going to talk about now come from this first one.

The next principle that comes from the first one is **KALA**. Kala, which says, **There are no limits**. Meaning that we are all connected. Each one of us is connected, mind and body, spirit and man, earth and plants and animals and clouds and sky and ocean. We are all one, we are all connected together.

Now Kala also says that separation is an illusion, but that because we can create our own reality with our thoughts, we sometimes create a sense, a belief in separation. And that as we believe we are separate, we create sickness. When the mind is separate from the body, when we think these two are separate, then in that way we create sickness.

When the body, our body, ourselves are separate from the people around us, when we create that kind of separation in our thoughts and our feelings, then there is sickness in our relationships. When we feel we are separate from the earth, that the earth is a thing outside of us, then we get sick, and so does the earth. But Kala says that there is really, underneath all of that sense of separation, a real oneness. And that if we can get rid of those ideas and feelings and acts and behaviors and thoughts of separation, that oneness comes together. That connection is made again, we become healthy and whole within ourselves and with the world around us. This is Kala—it is a way of creating that connection again, a freeing up.

You've probably seen in Hawaii, a gesture they do which says, 'Hang Loose!' And the meaning is very clear, it means that when you get uptight, when you create tension, then you create separation. So when you hang loose, when you relax, when you allow things to flow, you are healthier, relationships with everything are better, and a very interesting thing happens. When you are relaxed and flowing with things, it is easier to change them. So Kala is not saying that you must accept things the way they are, forever, without changing; it says that when you relax with them, you can change them easier. That's Kala.

The third idea that these wise people discovered was called **MAKIA** (mah-kee-ah). Makia, that **Energy flows where attention goes**. Wherever there is a flow of energy and attention, events are created. And wherever you direct your attention, and keep it directed in that way, to an object or to an idea, then the flow of energy carries. And according to the nature of your thoughts, that's the return flow that you get. So that if you're putting out and thinking very positive thoughts about the world around you, then positive energy flows back. And that when you are putting out and thinking negative thoughts about the world around you, then negative energy flows back, negative results come into your life. If you are putting our thoughts of abundance, and keeping that consistently, not just once in a while, but thinking that way, then abundance flows into your life. If you are thinking thoughts of happiness and joy, consistently, then to that degree happiness and joy flow back into your life. And where you focus on fear and anger, then you have fear and anger in your life. Where you focus on violence and upsetting and illness, then violence and upsetting and illness flow into your life.

You have the ability, the wonderful skill, says this knowledge, of deciding how you are going to focus your thoughts, your energy, your attention, and thereby change what is flowing back into your life. So all of these principles of this knowledge, starting from the first one, are telling you how to make the changes from within that will make the changes from outside.

There is a fourth idea, called **MANAWA** (man-ah-wah). Manawa is the idea that **Now is the moment of power**. This moment, right here. That there is no power in the past, no power in the future. That the past has no power over you either. That you are the one that has power right in this moment to change what you think, and then the past, and the effects of the past, fail to hold you. You walk forward in life from moment to moment with ideas about yourself and about the past. And it is those ideas, in every given moment, that create your reality. If there is beauty in your life, as we have beauty in these Hawaiian Islands, then you are creating that beauty now. Says this idea, you increase that beauty by enjoying and appreciating that beauty now. If you stop appreciating that beauty, if you start losing your sense of beauty, then so does the land around you lose its beauty, as we have seen happens some places on this earth of ours. But the more you appreciate, take pleasure in the moment, the more you strengthen that, the more you increase that.

So it is not what you've been, but what you are, that makes what you have in any given moment. And the future, as well, does not lie in front of you, waiting for you to move forward and bump into it. The future is created in every present moment by the seeds of thought that you plant now. Sometimes we have weeds from the past, but we can pull those up now, and plant new seeds, and create a new future. So says this knowledge. As we go along, new seeds are planted, and if we decide that we don't like, at some moment, what these seeds have produced, then at any time, we can pull them up and plant new seeds. So it is every moment that we have our power, and there is power in everything else too, in every present moment.

One of the most wonderful ideas of this knowledge comes in a word that you've already heard, which is **ALOHA**. Aloha, which is so often taken to mean hello and good-bye. And it is used that way. We speak of the spirit of aloha which is so often taken to mean friendship. And it is friendship. But it is more. More than friendship, more than hello and good-bye, Aloha means love. Pure and simple, this is the meaning of that beautiful word. Love.

And even deeper within the word is the meaning of love, which is **To be happy with**. To be happy with something or someone, this is the great discovery, the most marvelous secret of this knowledge that was discovered by these people. That to love is to be happy with. To the degree that you are happy with yourself, with other people, with the world around you, you are in love. And love is being expressed, and love is flowing. But to the degree that you are criticizing, to the degree that you have anger, are not pleased with, do not like things in people around you, you reduce and diminish love. So that love has nothing to do with pain. Love has nothing to do with hurting people or being hurt. Love is the happiness in any relationship. Love is the happiness and the joy and the friendship and the pleasure in any relationship. Because to love is to be happy with.

The sixth principle is **MANA**. Mana is a word that has been often misunderstood, taken to mean energy alone. But Mana is an idea that means power, divine power, creative power. The concept of Mana is that there is one source of all power, and that source flows through each one of us. Not only us as human beings, but through the earth itself, through every stone, through every tree, through every cloud. Mana is the inner power that give every thing its own creativity. Mana is the power of the waves, of the sea to come up and kiss the shore. Mana is the power of the wind to carry the clouds and the birds, and blow across the lands and the ocean. Mana is the power of a stone to be strong and and stable. Mana is the power of human beings to be creative, in their own unique way. Mana is that source of power within each person, within each thing in this universe.

Now, most important from this comes the further idea that **All power comes from within**. This is the principle, meaning that there is no power outside of you that has any power over you. That all the power for your existence comes from that one source through you. That whenever we think that something else has power, whether it is nature, or whether it is another person, whether it is spirit, whatever it is that we think has more power over our lives than we do, all we are doing, according to this knowledge, is diminishing our own power, holding it back, holding it down. And in a very strange way pretending not to have the power we really have.

Now Mana is a power to do something, to be creative, not a power over. So it is that inner power within each thing, within each person to be itself, and to be itself to its utmost potential. Now the more we allow ourselves to experience that power, to feel it, to use it, to claim it, then we have that power to make ourselves match our highest potential.

There is a seventh principle, called **PONO**, and it says that **Effectiveness is the of truth**. That there is always another way to do anything. That we are never really stuck in one way, that there is no one way for anything. That there is no one truth, that there is no one method, one technique, one kind of medicine, one way to heal, one way to be happy, that there is only one person with whom you can be happy. There are many, many ways to achieve your goals, to be happy, to enjoy life, to fulfill it. This is Pono. That there is always another way to do anything.

The idea continues with the idea that plans are not sacred. Your purpose might be sacred, but the way you achieve that purpose is not. If you want to achieve a given purpose, however, you must use the means suitable to that purpose. If you want to create peace, then you must create peaceful means. For you will never get peace with violence. From violence you will only get more violence, until someday people may tire of the violence and get together and use peaceful means to create peace. But if you start out with peace in your heart, with a love of peace, says this knowledge, then you will move toward peace in your life. A very, very practical truth this one is. A very practical way of living, with yourself, and with other people.

These are the principles of this knowledge. Practiced by the Kapua, this knowledge called Kahuna, this knowledge that comes from these islands and others like them in the Pacific. Here is wisdom to share. And if you would share this, if you would use this, take any part of it that you choose, that you like, and apply and use it in your own life.

This is the end of my story. May you be blessed with peace and love, power and wisdom. Aloha!

"From the faraway, nearby." - Georgia O'Keefe

"How To Get Everything You Want Out Of Life"

BY EARL SHOAFF

This transcript derived from Shoaff's only known surviving speech, given in 1962.

I JUST WANT TO TAKE a few moments and cover some things that have assisted me in acquiring things in my life.

I know that few people are aware of these basic fundamental laws that operate in this world of ours. Some people are aware of them; some people are not aware of them, but they are using them. And sometimes we wonder why certain things happen to us, we acquire certain things and then over a period of time it seems like we live in stagnation. Nothing happens; nothing takes place; everything seems to be at a standstill.

There are basic laws in this universe that we are governed by and will work for you if you know how to apply them. And I would like to cover a couple of these laws that will assist you in knowing why these things happen.

For an example, everybody is aware of the law of gravitation. Now, we don't know how it works, but we know it works. It works for everybody. It doesn't matter whether you are a saint or whether you are the opposite of a saint. If you jumped off a 20-story building and you are a saint and you land on a concrete sidewalk, you are going to be an unhealthy saint. If you happen to be a crook and you do the same thing, the same thing happens to you. So basically, it doesn't matter if you are good or bad—if you use the law of gravity wrong you are going to suffer.

The law of electricity works for all of us. If we use it properly, we can light our homes by screwing a light bulb into a socket. If we stick our finger into it, then we get bit. You're going to get burned. We can burn your house down with electricity or you can light your home with it. You can cook with it. You can use refrigeration—all the great things that electricity will do for us!

You do not have to be an electrical-minded person. You don't have to be a genius to do it. A child three years old can push a button and turn the lights on. And one of the greatest electrical engineers in the world, all he can do when he pushes that button is that he can turn the lights on, too. So basically, it does not matter. It will work for you. We have laws to success.

We have laws of poverty. We have laws of lack, laws of prosperity. We have laws of hate. We have laws of love. We have laws of peace. All of these are basic laws. If we use them rightfully, wonderful things will happen to us. If we use them wrong, then we get ourselves in trouble.

Now, one of the things that has always bothered me, in all the books I've ever read on setting goals in life, positive thinking, positive goals in life—many of you have probably read some of the books—you follow these different steps, rules, laws, that if we set 10 goals we end up with 2. We lose out on 8. So it is not like the law of gravity seemingly, because it doesn't work every time. And one of the reasons it does not work every time, is that we do not use the right law. We are using part of the law, and so the law of averages will give you a percentage of your goals. That is all.

You say, "Gee, wasn't that great? It happened to me." But whatever happened to all the other goals you had in life?

I'M GOING TO LAY DOWN a simple basic way and you can have anything material you want to have and you can be anything you want to be, and it's a simple basic situation. There's absolutely no problem to it. These are scientific things that work every time if you will do it in a simple way.

Now, the first thing we want to become aware of is we want to be like farmers. We are going to plant seeds, and these seeds that we plant are the seeds that we're going to reap. Now we're all aware that if we plant a seed of tomatoes, we are not going to get cucumbers—we're going to get tomatoes. If you plant a watermelon seed, you're not going to get grapefruit. You're not going to get radishes. If you want radishes, folks, you're going to have to plant radish seeds. And when you plant a seed in the earth, you must plant it properly. If you do not plant it properly, you will not have the harvest. One of the major problems in our country today for the average person is they take the time and the effort to buy all the harvesting equipment, but they do not understand the planting and the cultivating.

We want to reap harvest, but we do not want to take the time to plant, and we do not want to take the time to cultivate. Now the planting of the seeds in the earth is basically and absolutely the same process that you use in the mental world.

We are born with a conscious mind and a sub-conscious mind. We are the only animal in the kingdom that have both the conscious and the sub-conscious mind—a mind that can decide anytime in life where we want to go or what we want or what we don't want. We can decide with this accomplished mind of ours if we want to do a thing or if we don't want to do a thing. We can decide if we want to eat or if we don't want to eat. We can decide if we want a drink, or if we don't want a drink. We can decide what we want in life in a home, in an automobile, in the clothes we wear, anything that we want in this world—any type of furniture, any type of a home, any type of an anything.

We decide at anytime. Now, where most people are making mistakes is that they simply set their goals down. Now, what are your goals? Write them down. A fellow says, I want a house, a car, some furniture, I want some money. And this is the way they set their goals.

Now he has a whole group of seeds, let's say apple seeds. We had 50 different types of apple seeds, and we just grabbed any of those seeds and we throw them in the ground and they come up and they're green apples. I wanted red ones. That's because you picked any type of an apple seed. You didn't describe it. So we must learn to define.

―――――――

NOW, YOU'VE HEARD OF the word "visualizing". You have to learn to visualize things. And when you visualize something, this is the thing that's going to come in your life, if the visualization is strong enough. Now we're always visualizing things in our life, but the tendency is to visualize negative situations. Now the reason that we're visualizing negative situations in our life is because, let's not kid ourselves, we're living in a negative world.

So if I say, "Joe, how are you feeling today?" And he says, "Good, fine." And I ask him the next day how he feels, and he says, "I feel terrible. I've got a pain in my stomach and I ache all over." And he goes into a...you'd think he was an actor. He can describe a negative situation in his body so wonderfully. But when he feels good, he just says, "Fine." How come people, when they feel fine, they don't say, "I feel great; I feel wonderful; I feel so great that I expect all the wonderful things in the world to happen to me today!"?

In other words, have a little feeling when you talk about the good things in life. I say, "How are you doing in business?" You say, "Fine." Now if he has a bad day, he says when I ask him about his day, "Lousy, let me tell you this is a...I'm just having a terrible time. Did you read that article the other day? It took me several hours to find it; it was on the back page down at the bottom in fine print, but I located it."

People love negative things. They seem to vibrate with them. For some strange reason, they don't want things that are negative in their life, but they keep insisting on talking about them. And they can paint the most beautiful picture of lost and lack.

I say by the way, "Internal..." and everybody immediately starts shaking..."combustion." A guy says, "You know what I thought you were going to say?" And he starts creating pictures and he says, by the way, I wonder about last year, what I did with that...I wonder if they'll find that...and immediately he says, I can see the guy coming in the door now...I wonder when he'll be here...I wonder what he'll look like... and he gets beautiful pictures, and the next thing you know, the guy is knocking on his door. He created the picture and he brought it into his life.

———

AND THE FUNNY THING ABOUT creating things, folks: we are creators. Nothing comes to us. Everything comes through us from us. Everything in this world that happens to us comes from in here, not out there.

And everything that you have in your life is exactly what you designed, the dress you're wearing, the coat you're wearing, the tie you're wearing, the necklace you're wearing, the home you're living in, the neighbors you've got, the friends you've got and the Senators you've got.

So don't blame me for people that you attracted! When you signed this person up, you're the guy that coached them in. You didn't care who it was as long as he came in. And pretty soon, you helped plenty of them and you say, "You know what, Shoaff? I've got a lousy bunch of distributors."

Well, when you understand these laws, you won't tell me these things. I'm not talking about you, or you—I wouldn't dare. There's too many here. What I am saying is that everything we attract is what we are, and what I am speaks so loudly I can't hear what you say. And what you are speaks so loudly I cannot hear what you say. So everything you say is the thing that you created. So be careful what you create. Be careful. It's hard to visualize a thing.

Let's try something, folks. Let's visualize a 707, shall we? What's a 707 look like? I've only been in one a couple of times. I've only seen one in the air once. It's hard to visualize one. You want to visualize an automobile, or a stole? I don't know why I keep saying "stole."

My wife must be visualizing a stole. I keep getting that feeling...every time we come to New York. You see, we have to learn how to describe things. Now I'm going to go through a description of a thing because this is very important in your life, folks. Please try to remember what I'm saying. You can change your life that quick. You can have everything wonderful in your life; you can have everything wonderful happening to you, if you use these few basic little things.

Now I'm going to describe a thing—an automobile. I'll talk about an automobile because an automobile is easy to describe, and people can comprehend it very quickly and very easily. I'm not going to talk about a Chevrolet; I'm going to talk about a Cadillac. Anytime I'm talking about a Cadillac, folks, I'm not describing the Cadillac per se; I'm talking about a Cadillac idea—the Cadillac idea in the clothing, in the home and the things you really desire deep within you. And I'm not talking about something that you say. "Well, I've got to have money to buy a Cadillac." I'm not talking about money. It's not necessary that you have money to have a Cadillac. There are many wonderful things that can happen to you. These things can come to you from many unusual sources. Many wonderful things can happen to you.

If you believe in the thing I'm talking about, your income can be doubled, tripled, quadrupled. The one thing that I had in my mind, that I had defined in my mind, was a red Cadillac convertible. I never had owned a Cadillac in my life. Now you probably don't want a red Cadillac. I wanted one, and I defined that thing right down to the socks, and the end result was I had me a red Cadillac convertible, and my income increased to a point where it cost me nothing. This is visualizing. This is a positive attitude toward the things you want.

Too many people stop their dreams because they start thinking about that thing that is not necessary in order to have it. I say to somebody, "Do you want a new Cadillac?" You say, "I want one, but I can't afford it." I say, "It has nothing to do with affording. I just want to know what you really want."

Most people are afraid to define what they want in life. They're afraid it's going to cost them something. Well if you're making $1,000 a month right now, and you double your income to $2,000 per month, you can have a Cadillac, you can have two Cadillacs, you can have five Cadillacs. Don't worry about the income—I'm just talking about the principle now. The Cadillac—what do you do about it? I'll say, "Pete, what would you like to have?" He says, "A Cadillac." Now don't forget folks, I'm going to give it to him—I'm going to give it to him. He has nothing to worry about—no money, no nothing. I say, "Pete, what do you want?" He says, "A Cadillac." I say, "Fine, Pete."

Now this is where people make their mistakes. I say, "I've got a nice 1936 beat-up model downstairs. I'll give it to you." He says, "I don't want a 1936 model Cadillac." I said, "You just told me you wanted a Cadillac." He says, "I want a '62 Cadillac." I said, "Why didn't you tell me, Pete? Why didn't you tell me?" This is the way people set their dreams. He doesn't just want a Cadillac. Do you want an orange or a green one? He says, "I want a red one."

Now he's starting to define. And you know it's very difficult to define up here in your mind. The first thing you do is you get a piece of paper folks, and you start defining on a piece of paper. A 1962 Cadillac, a red Cadillac, a convertible—I'm just describing one car now. You can have any kind of car you want—a red Cadillac, 1962 convertible with a white top, red/white upholstery, a red floor, white wall tires, electric windows, a/c unit. The guy says, "How much does that cost?" I say, "Don't worry bout it—you're going to get it for nothing." The guy says, "I'll take it, then." Now he says, "I'm going to put everything down then." That's right—describe it right down to the tee.

And when he gets all through, the perfect visualization is up here now because he has described it. When you write it, you start seeing it. He gets the picture up here by writing it down here. This is how you define things that you want in this world. When he gets that Cadillac completely defined in his mind, he's got the seed. He hasn't planted it yet. He's just got it picked out.

NOW THE IMPORTANT THING is that you must release that seed. You must release it and it must be planted. And the perfect thing in the world to plant that seed is to take this piece of paper now and write the concept, "Thank you". That's the law of acceptance. And you would be amazed how many people in this world can't accept their goods. You would be shocked. "Thank you" means you have accepted it. "I'm going to have it. I know it's mine." Then you take and you fold this piece of paper up with this goal on it, with this dream, with this desire and you put it away—put it underneath a tablecloth some place, put it in a drawer some place. Don't carry it around and don't take it out and look at it anymore. When you do this, that is planting it in the subconscious mind.

You've accepted—you've put it into the subconscious mind, and the thing starts to work. Now when you put this thing away, the reason you put it away after you have defined it: the seed has been planted in the subconscious mind. You put it away some place, never to be looked at again. The reason for it is like planting a seed in the earth, folks. If you go and dig that seed up two or three times a day to look at it, nothing is going to happen.

If you've never seen a lack of faith—it's the farmer who had the gullibility to dig up the seed to see if it was growing yet. Now that is little faith. He really believes in the laws of growth, and that's the same way with us human beings. This is the way we're making our mistakes. When we plant in the subconscious mind, and it's there, the dream is there. The dream starts working towards you, the Cadillac starts working towards you, and events start taking place out here, and the next thing you know it's getting closer and closer to you.

Now if you take it out, and you start to look at it, the thing that happens is we say, "I wonder where it's coming from." This is a true showing of a lack of faith. "I wonder when it's coming. I wonder how it's coming." And so you are putting doubt in your law, and it will not come, folks. It will not come to you.

Now, what's going to happen to the seed that you planted in the subconscious mind: you'll be driving down the street, you'll be in a restaurant talking to a friend and all of a sudden, there's a red Cadillac convertible with a white top and the whole thing will hit you again and you'll see your dream. And it'll keep coming back.

The reason it'll keep coming back to you is this is the only way that the universal law has of talking to you. There's no voice—it's all in visualization. And when this dream comes up, what it really means is that's it's on its way to you. It is on its way to you—it's right around the corner. And so you do not at that time say, "How, when or where." All you do is say, "Thank you" because you know it's on its way. And then immediately put it back out of your mind.

And how would you act if you really and truly wanted a red Cadillac convertible—if you really and truly wanted one and it was a strong desire in your life, and you knew it was on its way, how would you act? You'd be excited, wouldn't you? You'd feel good—you'd say, "Man it's almost here, it's almost here." You'd walk taller, you'd look taller. You'd be happier. You'd be full of positive. You'd act different. Wonderful things are going to happen to you.

Where does the positive attitude come in at? It automatically creates a positive attitude because it's the law of expectancy. Good things are going to happen. You have planted your seeds properly, and they are working themselves to you, and you are automatically a positive person because all these wonderful things are going to happen. Don't just have one seed planted, folks—plant many seeds—any great desire you have in your life—a tangible object or intangible object. You can have anything in this world you want to have and you can be anything in this world you want to be by using this simple process.

THERE IS ABSOLUTELY NO WAY you can keep success from your door, if you will just follow this basic, simple little process that

I just described. This is the law of life, and every one of you people have worked this process. Maybe you weren't completely aware of how you worked it.

But think about it—that's why you only get 3 out of 8 things, or 1 out of 8 or 1 out of 10, because you didn't know exactly the process you were using. Now you know the process, so you can deal with anything in this world. Children—our children, folks. How many times have you heard people say to their children when the child says, "I'm going to be President of The United States," and the father and mother will say to them, "You? With your studies, you'll never make it, Junior." Now this is a wonderful seed to plant in that fertile little brain. The subconscious is putting in the mind—telling him he can't; he's not smart enough.

The child says, "I'm going to be a rich man when I grow up. I'm going to have everything in this world." You say, "You? You're going to have to learn a lot, junior. You don't know how to handle money. You've got to learn how to use that ol' elbow grease." Anybody who's ever used much elbow grease, if he's ever made millions, I'll assure you the elbow grease is up here.

Now, what do you want to tell Junior? Anytime any children come to you or to their parents, you should tell your children, "Junior, you're the type of child who can have anything in this world. You have the ability and the intelligence to go anywhere, do anything and have everything in this world.

It is yours because you're that type of a child. Start planting these seeds in our children. This country today is teaching too many children, too many children, what to think instead of how to think.

And what are we? We are only children a little older than the other children. We are grown-up children, and we have to at some time in life, we have to start deciding and pinpointing things that we want in this world. And I'm not just talking about the tangible objects. I'm talking about intangible things.

What would you like to be? What type of person would you like to be? Would you like to have more love in your life? Well then, you must learn to give love. You'll never have anything without giving. Everything I have I receive back, multiplied. If I have a lot of hate in my life, I'm giving a lot of hate out.

And so if I don't want hate coming in my life, I shouldn't be giving it out. If I don't want people to talk about me, I shouldn't be talking about people. Everything that I send out, I get back with feeling. Every thought I think I don't get, because I didn't plant my seed properly—I did not have a true visualization.

How many of you ladies have thought of a beautiful dress or a beautiful something that you don't have. How many would love to have a mink stole? A few years ago, if my wife even mentioned a mink stole, the first thing that would come in my mind was, "Where are you going to get it from? How are you going to pay for it?" I did not understand these things. When you just say, "mink stole," do you know what?

I never was aware that there was so many mink stoles in this country—every kind of every price and color and designs and everything else, and if you don't even know the exact kind you want, how do you know if you can ever expect to have it? Do you know the amazing thing? The average person in this world, and I'm only saying this because we are the average people of the world, and I say average because I am talking to an intelligent group of people. I'm not talking to people way down the ladder. I'm talking to a group of intelligent people. And I'm saying this, and you analyze this yourself.

Ask yourself this basic question. Do you know what you want in life? If I were to ask you right now, "What do you really want? What is a tangible object that you want in this world—things you can feel and touch and smell?

What are the things you want in life? And you know, folks, the amazing thing—I doubt if there's 2% of the people in this room who can tell me and describe it, and just like that come right out and say it. So, what is success in your life? What is it that you want? Define it. Write it down. Pinpoint every drop of that dream that you have in your mind. Define it so clearly on that piece of paper that you can completely see it in your mind. And when you get it written down, write "thank you" on it and plant that seed and put it away, and it will start to materialize and it will start coming into your life.

That is anything folks, anything.

Now a guy says, "I'm going to put down The Statler Hotel." You know why it wouldn't work for him? I'm not saying it won't work for the fellow, but I am saying that it won't work for the average person. Do you know why? He couldn't even imagine getting it. He can write it down. He can define it, and he can put "thank you" on it, but he can never plant the seed.

And the reason he can't is because he couldn't even imagine getting The Statler Hotel, that's why. And don't forget, this is something you have to accept—you're going to have it, folks. I told people about a Cadillac, average people working on average jobs. I said, "Do you want a Cadillac?" The guys said, "No, no, I don't want no Cadillac." I said, "Well, why don't you want a Cadillac?" He said, "For one thing, it cost so much to operate them." You see, he doesn't want one—he isn't ready for that step yet.

Now see, he steps from one car to another to another. He raises his consciousness, until pretty soon, he can buy Cadillacs like the average person buys a pair of shoes. And you can grow; you can grow in your thinking. People say, "Boy, you got to be careful about people—they'll take you in if you're not careful." They get such a wonderful visualization—they're always getting taken in. So you see how we build these pictures in our mind? People will spend the morning; they're going to get ready for a wonderful day.

Tomorrow morning, we're getting ready for a wonderful day; we're going out and it's going to be the most exceptional day we've ever had in our entire lives. I said, "How are you going to start the morning? Exactly what are you going to do?" He says, "Well, the first thing I'm going to do is go out on the porch." He's going through his morning now—he's going to go out on his porch and get his newspaper and read a little bit about positive thinking in the headlines.

And if he can't find it there, he'll look and look and look and look until he finds something that is really good and negative and then he'll tell his wife and describe it, and he says, "Guess what I found in the paper?" And he starts telling her about some wonderful divorce that's taken place in the paper and the kids committed suicide, and he'll go on with this and he'll say, "Just imagine that, imagine that!"

And he'll describe it, and the negativity will get started and the wife will get negative and he will get more negative and when he gets all through with breakfast now, he's in such a nasty mood that he doesn't even like his dog! And he's going out to face the world with a positive attitude.

Do you see how ridiculous it is folks—some of the ridiculous things we do in life and we wonder why success doesn't always come to us in the proportion we'd like to have it come to us?

EXPECT WONDERFUL THINGS. Be a creator of ideas.

Let's not be moons, the reflector of ideas. Let's be suns, let's be the creator of the light; let's be the creator of the ideas, because we all have a capacity—that guardian of the gate, as the conscious mind. This guardian can at any time let any thought through to the subconscious mind it wants—any thought at any time.

We are thinking human beings. We have the capacity to think of anything, anything in this world we can think of, but we do not have the capacity to think of nothing. Now you try to imagine what nothing is. Try to get a thought of that—there is absolutely no way. So that means we are thinking human beings and there are thoughts flying through our mind continuously—a steady flow of thoughts all the time coming through the mind.

Now where do these thoughts come from? All of a sudden, you say, "Gee, that thought must have come out of the clear blue sky." You didn't think of it, and it might have been something you didn't even know about. And the thought comes through and you say, "Well, that's kind of ridiculous, isn't it? That couldn't happen to me." And so you throw that thought aside. And if it's a good thought, why not accept it? Stop and analyze it and accept it. And let them happen to you.

And these objects come through to you all the time. A negative thought comes through and you say, "Boy, that's a good and negative thought and you start thinking about it and pretty soon you get a frown on your face and you think about it a little bit more and you create a beautiful picture and all of a sudden you put that down in the subconscious and you think, "Boy, there's another bad thing that's going to happen to me."

Have you ever caught yourself thinking about something you didn't want to think about and you've been thinking about it for 5 minutes and all of a sudden you think, "What am I thinking about that nasty thing for?" We do it; we do it all the time, folks.

But we can stop now, any time we want, and we can change that thought and we can put in a good thought. If you don't want to think about oranges, change the thought and think about bananas, if you want. If you don't want to think about lack, change the thought and think about prosperity. If you don't want to think about hate, think about love.

If you don't want to think of anything negative, put a positive idea in your head. You know what happens, you can analyze and you can just dream about it and everything else, and get all these seeds planted properly and have all these wonderful things happen. Get twenty wonderful seeds planted, get them written down. Define. Thank you. Plant them into the subconscious mind.

Put it away, and every time it comes back into the subconscious mind and the law saying it's on its way, you just say "Thank you". Don't analyze it because it's already planted. Just say "Thank you" and go on.

Have ten, fifteen, twenty, thirty of these wonderful seeds planted and folks, you'll walk on air. You'll have miracles happen in your life. And don't be afraid to do this. Your wife isn't in harmony with the wonderful things you want to happen to you; well, if the husband isn't in harmony or if the children are not, or your friends aren't, you don't have to show them.

Plant your seeds privately then, and put them away privately and plant them deep and all these wonderful things will happen and you'll say, "You know, one thing about that person, I don't know what happened to him, but man oh man, everything they touch turns to gold.

And that's the reason. That's the reason, folks—the proper planting of your seeds.

If You Can Count to Four...

BY J. B. JONES

Excerpted from the first chapter of Jones' bestseller "If You Can Count to Four..."

————————

IF YOU CAN COUNT TO four, you can learn a simple set of rules which will unlock the treasures of the universe in all its dimensions.

Millions of people have been taught to believe that the rules of success are indeed so very difficult and complicated that surely they could never learn them.

The average person is perfectly willing to accept the fact that several hundred families in most any community are successful. They, at the same time, know that there are hundreds of communities in our own country and, of course, and all the other countries too.

If they would stop and think for a moment, they would also know that when you add up the hundreds in each community, and then multiply by the thousands of communities all over the world, that it would add up to hundreds of thousands of people who are very successful.

For example, not long ago it was my pleasure to visit Mexico City. I was surprised to learn that there are approximately 10,000 millionaires in Mexico City. We hear of the millions of extremely poor people in the country of Mexico. But, at the same time, there are 10,000 millionaires in just one city in Mexico. How could there be that many rich people and millions of poor people unless there is a basic system of rules that 10,000 of them are using and the millions are not using? I too, wondered about these perplexing problems for many years.

I was born into a family of 14 children down in the hills of Tennessee and the first 18 years of my life I was what was considered a poor boy. I observed hundreds of families who obviously were not poor. They had poise, culture, a feeling of well-being, self-confidence, a measure of health, and they had plenty of money to express life abundantly. I wondered why my wonderful parents did not have those things in abundance too. I was stirred to investigate and find out, if possible, the answer to this problem.

I found out that anyone can be genuinely successful if he will learn the exact same "rules" that the successful people learned and use them.

To be genuinely successful, to me, is to enjoy a large measure of happiness, health and prosperity. It is a balanced type of life; Harmonious living with good physical health and also plenty of money.

So, it was my privilege to start out as a poor, unhappy person and to make the same observations that the millions are now making. It was my privilege to learn these basic rules and to take them out into the hard-boiled business world and to challenge every one of them. *And to discover, beyond any shadow of a doubt, that there not only is a system of rules, but that anyone, not just a few, can learn them and use them and become just as successful as he wants to be.*

The title of this section, "If You Can Count to Four" is designed to tell you that regardless of your background, your lack of education, your lack of knowing anyone who is supposed to be important, your lack of funds, or any other seeming lack, you can still be what you want to be and have what you want to have.

Yes, you can start right now without funds, without education, without friends or influence, without an idea, without anything but a sincere desire to be somebody expressing life, and you can be that person you have secretly always wanted to be, and you can have all the money you want to express yourself within every field of your own choosing.

Are you ready to put The Count to Four technique into action? I am sure that you are. I know that you are because I know that you have many desires which you have never realized.

It has been said that 98 people out of every 100 have never decided just exactly what they want to be in life. That is, they have never come to any decision regarding a "life's goal" like Henry Ford, Thomas Edison or Andrew Carnegie. But here is the most important thing as far as I am concerned. It is understood that 98 out of every hundred haven't made that big decision, but I happen to know, and you do too, that you and I and every other person living at this moment has some desire, right at this moment, that we want to realize as soon as possible.

Ask yourself the question, "What do I want to be next?" "What do I want to attain next?" List all the things you want to be next and all the things you want to have next. Let's not worry too much about what we want next year or five years from now or 20 years from now, at this point. If you have just one little desire right now that you wish fulfilled and you don't know exactly how to go about it, then you are ready to learn how to "Count to Four".

––––––––

LET'S BEGIN BY LOOKING at *Phase One* which is to *identify what you want.*

Write it down.

Define it.

Describe it.

There are several ways of helping your subconscious mind to become deeply impressed with exactly what you want. For example, you can cut pictures out of magazines and paste them in a scrapbook. If you can draw well, or if you know a friend who is an artist, you can create drawings or pictures of your idea of what you want.

By going through this simple mental process, your subconscious mind is impressed with exactly what you want. I want to point out, right at this point, that what I am asking you to do does not cost you one red penny. I merely want you to do it so that we can cause your mind to go through certain "thoughts."

You see your thoughts as size and color and texture. One of the reasons a person is living a small, limited type of life now is that he is in the habit of thinking small, limited thoughts. So, for Phase One, *let's not ask the price.*

Let's just identify what we really want. It can be any size and color and texture and design. At this point, all we are concerned with is "a mental process" which does not cost a cent. So, do what I am asking you to do, because if you will, I guarantee you that you will realize your desire in every case.

So, with the humility of a little child, get yourself a notebook and write down everything that you want to be next and everything that you want to have next. First of all, just write them down in your own words so that you can read them and they will cause you to know what you want next.

Then, after you have written these things down, start cutting out the pictures which represent what you want and paste them in the notebook. For example, I have done this in regard to automobiles, and I have known many of my students to do the same. I decide that I want a certain automobile, then I write it down in my notebook. I go down to the dealer and obtain as many color pictures as possible and then I paste one of them in my notebook, on the wall by my bed, in the bathroom by the mirror and in my desk, so that every time I open the drawer I see the picture of what I want.

By doing all these things I accomplish the purpose of the ONE phase of of the formula of success. *I developed a keen, clear, distinct mental picture of exactly what I want.* The subconscious will help us obtain exactly what we want or if we give it a hazy, unclear, smeared concept or mental picture, it will help us obtain that.

Which would you rather have, just exactly what you want or a smeared, unclear approximation of what you want? I can tell you from hundreds of experiences that this works right down to a "T."

I might say here, that of the thousands of successful people whom I have studied, every one of them had either consciously or unconsciously developed the ability to think distinctly and clearly, and to define and identify the things which they wanted.

The millions of people who do not have the things they want, at the same time, have not developed their ability to think clearly. Yes, they had the same basic ability to learn to think distinctly as anybody, but they did not realize that it was important or that it had anything to do with him getting what they wanted, so they just continued to think in a blurred, indistinct manner.

When I found this out in my research I was deeply impressed and immediately started trying to think more clearly. I began to identify exactly what I wanted to be and have. I noticed right away, a change in my life. I had more of a feeling of harmony and peace as soon as

I took charge of my thoughts and started to define distinctly what I wanted to be and have. Also, my financial situation began to get better and better.

Most of you will say at this point, "Well, I can certainly accomplish Phase One." As long as it doesn't cost anything, what have I got to lose? You say to yourself, "If there is just one remote possibility that this will work, even though I do not quite understand just how it works, I am certainly going to get started right away and obtain a nice notebook, and write down my secret dreams of what I have always wanted to be and I am making a complete list of everything I want of a material nature.

"Since all he is asking me to do at this point, is to go through the mental activity, the least I can do is cooperate with him, as he promises me that I can be what I want to be and that I can have what I want to have. I am approaching this with just simple childlike faith as he has tested in his own life and many thousands of others and it has never failed.

"I don't have to understand just how it works, anymore than I have to understand the way my television set works in order to enjoy it fully; or anymore than I have to be an electrician in order to enjoy all the fine things which I enjoy through electricity. I must assume that there are 'laws' about which Dr. Jones is familiar, and he is sharing with me a simple little,one, two, three, four routine, which, if I follow, I can enjoy the full benefit of as though I understood it fully.

"I know that even little child can just turn on a light switch and not know anything about how it works, and all the lights will burn just as well for the child as if an expert electrician had turned on the light switch."

I must say just one more thing before I take you into the next phase which is Phase Two. I know that most of you will believe in this enough to try it. I congratulate you, because when you try it, you will find that it works.

And, of course, you will become what you want to be and you will have what you want to have. But there will be a few who think that they are so smart, that they will say, "Ah, that Jones guy is crazy." I would like to challenge you, if you should fall into this type.

Go ahead and prove me wrong. You can never honestly say that it won't work unless you try it and see whether it works or not. Go ahead, try it and prove me wrong. I have a pleasant surprise for you. You will end up being what you want to be in having what you want to have.

═══════════

NOW, LET'S MOVE TO Phase Two.

Phase Two *is also just a mental exercise, and it doesn't cost you one red penny. Phase Two is as follows:* "Pretend" that you already are what you want to be, and that you already have what you want to have.

Ask yourself, "How would I feel if I were already the person I want to be? If I already had the things that I have written down on my Phase One list, how would I feel? What would I do? Where would I be right now?" In other words, assume the fulfilled dream.

Assume the feeling of the dream fulfilled. When a farmer plants a field of corn, he cultivates it, rains fall on it and the sun shines on it and it grows and grows until one day it is ready for the harvest. You see, Phase One of this formula is like planting the seed. Phase Two is like watering, cultivating and warming the soil by the sun shining on it. When you "pretend" that you are the person you want to be, you go through special mental activities or mental exercises which are like plowing the corn, or cultivating it.

When you assume the warm, deep emotional feeling of the person you want to be, it is like the warm sunshine shining on the growing corn. I can tell you many details of what actually takes place inside you and what happens in the whole universe, when you "pretend" but believe me, I know that if you will do it in simple childlike faith your dreams will come true. Is that fair enough at this point?

Later on, for those of you who are interested, I will be happy to go into the deeper aspects of the laws involved.

Someone will ask, "How do I comfortably go through these mental exercises of pretending that I am a certain person in my dreams?"

One of the best ways that I have ever used is as follows:

- I first assume that I have already attained my desire.
- Then I ask myself what event would normally take place after I had attained my desire but would never take place other than if I had attained my desire.
- Then I make arrangements to live that event as though I had already attained my desire.

For example, I went on the air on my first television program on June 19, 1955. I had my desire to be on television written down for several months before June, 1955. So, in March, 1955, I arranged an occasion to dramatize an event which would normally only take place after my first appearance on television. I arranged to have a debut party at my house, and the time was, as we pretend, the evening after I had debuted on TV that afternoon.

Each guest was invited and given a script, which told him exactly what to say at the party. So each guest arrived with great joy and enthusiasm congratulating me on having done a fine job that afternoon on my first telecast. All evening, our discussions were regarding how happy we all were that the program had been launched so well in the great good that would be done by the principles of genuine success being taken to so many hundreds of thousands of people, etc.

We pretend that we were celebrating the start of a television program in March, but the actual program did not start until June or about three months later. But we all assumed the mental attitude, the excited feeling, the tones of reality, of having already started the program. I happen to know that by doing this very thing it played a very important part in bringing my dream into fulfillment so soon.

You don't have to do anything great in order to use this one, two, three, four technique.

Let's suppose that your little girl wants a new tricycle. One day you see her riding an old broom around in the backyard. You ask her what she is doing and she says, "I'm riding my new red tricycle." She is using the same technique. She, first of all, did Phase One, which is to decide that she wanted a new red tricycle; then she was doing Phase Two by riding the broom and pretending that it was already her actual new red tricycle. It's just that simple. It doesn't cost a penny so far, and it's just a mental activity which you go through like a little child.

Let's suppose that you want to be a person who has great poise so that you can meet all life situations without fear or feeling of nervousness. You would even like to be able to stand up and speak before groups with poison comfort. Then, if that is what you want, you have your Phase One part already.

What about Phase Two? You would do several things. Every time you attend a group meeting in the person of poise gets up and gives a really good speech, you see yourself as being the person giving that speech. Get that feeling of giving that speech by pretending that you are the person giving it. Also, give a party and coach your guests and celebrate your having given a great speech the day before. Also, line up some chairs in your living room, and one day when no one is there but you, assume that all those chairs are full of people.

Stand up and talk to them as long as you can think of anything to say. It doesn't matter at this point, just keep standing there and keep talking about anything whatsoever, and after a while you will get a feeling of comfort and you will then begin to control your thoughts. Then, after awhile, you will find yourself taking advantage of every opportunity of accepting appointments to speak before groups and you will one day find that you are a person of poise and confidence.

It doesn't matter whether you want to be the President of the United States, and Ambassador to a foreign country, a Congressman, a Senator, a movie star, a great singer, a great industrialist, a great attorney, a great salesman, a great farmer, a great housewife and mother, a great secretary, or a great whittler, you can become anything you want to be, big or little, by applying this one, two, three, four technique.

Can you fulfill Phase Two? Sure you can. All you need is the desire and humility of a little child.

BUT PHASE THREE IS very important.

Phase Three is, "That ability within you to say, Yes and No."

Many people have not learned that it is their individual prerogative to evaluate any life situation or event or proposition and then down deep inside say, "Yes" if they believe it should be yes, and to say "No" if it should be no. I am not advising you whether, in certain circumstances, you should say "yes" or "no", but in order to emphasize this point, I would like to say that you have the power, and the right, and the ability, if you choose, to use it; and the God of Heaven gave you that power, right, and ability to use it.

Yes, you have within you the power, the right and the ability to look your father and mother right in the face and say "yes" or "no." You can look your minister right in the face and say "yes" or "no." You can look your husband, or your wife, right in the face and say "yes" or "no." You can look your friend, or your so-called enemy in the face and say "yes" or "no." Yes, you can look even God in the face and say "yes" or "no", because he gave you "dominion" and that means that you can say "yes" or "no" to every source of suggestion, even your God, and face the possibility of enjoying the results of having made the right decision, or of suffering from having made the wrong decision.

But the point I am making is that you were given the right, the power, and the intelligence, and the ability to learn to say, "yes" or "no."

Now, you have followed the suggestions made in Phase One and Phase Two very closely. But, one day you will happen to mention what you are doing, to a friend, your husband or your wife, your mother or father, your minister, and one or more of them immediately begins to make fun of you or discourage you. They tell you, "You mean that you fell for that!"; "Don't be silly"; "I don't believe that stuff, and I think that you are nuts"; or some sort of discouragement.

Well, Phase Three of this technique is "down deep inside you." Pay no attention to them whatsoever, but keep your thoughts on Phase One and Phase Two. Keep identifying your desires, and keep "living in the feeling of having already attained them." *Yes, you can control your attention units. You can learn to say "no" to anything which will hinder the fulfillment of your dreams.* You are the master of your fate, the captain of your soul!

Again, let me stress that so far it doesn't cost anything. When I lecture on the subject around the country I consistently have people ask me, "How much does it cost me to quit being what I am now and become what I want to be? How much does it cost me to get the things I want now?"

Well, I tell them that I had discovered and have proved a simple little technique that really works every time. It is called the "IF YOU CAN COUNT TO FOUR TECHNIQUE" Phase One doesn't cost one cent. Phase Two doesn't cost a cent. And Phase Three doesn't cost a cent either. And now, let me tell you that Phase Four doesn't cost a cent either. Is that fair enough?

PHASE FOUR IS THE HOW!

How do you get from here and now, to there, and what you want to be, and have what you want to have and not cost you anything?

Well, I am going to give you the answer in several ways so that you will be sure to trust it. First, let me say, that I am aware of certain facts, laws, rules, powers which are all natural, and which, if you will do certain things with the simple faith of a child, will all work for you and bring your dreams all fulfilled to you.

How many of you have ever had an idea come to you for "out of the blue?" All of you have, I am absolutely sure. Well, how many of you know just where the "blue" is located? I don't exactly know where it is located myself, but I know the name we give it.

The "blue" is your subconscious mind.

Now, your subconscious mind is like the "soil" into which the farmer plants seeds. The farmer plants for example, wheat. What grain does he expect to one day harvest? "Wheat, of course" you say. May I ask you "How does the farmer take one bushel of wheat, plant it in good soil and a few months later harvest, say 40 bushels? Where does the extra 39 bushels come from?" "Oh," you say, "Nature did it."

Well, the farmer has learned by experience that there is something, some power which he calls nature and that if he plants good seed in good soil in good season he can depend on this power in some manner or means which he does not completely understand to take his one bushel of wheat and increase it to 40 bushels.

At the same time, he knows this power does not steal this extra 39 bushels from the neighbor's granary. This power, in some fashion not fully understood takes just one bushel of seed, about an acre of soil, and about three or four months time.

The faith of the farmer, the warmth of the sun, the moisture of the rain, and other invisible elements, are combined and out of what appears to be "Nothingness" produces 40 new bushels of wheat. The farmer is pleased with the whole affair and his neighbor is not angry with him.

- Phase One is the seed.
- Phase Two is the watering, cultivating, sunshine and faith.
- Phase Three is keeping the weeds out and not letting the

enemy destroy your seed which has been well planted and is being cultivated until the harvest.

- Phase Four is the Subconscious Mind, which has the same quality in the field of LIFE as the soil has for the farmer.

In this way, the same as the soil takes one bushel of wheat and gives you forty fresh, new bushels of wheat, the subconscious takes one good idea,and through laws only known to itself, makes it into your dream fulfilled.

But you ask, "Just how are some of the ways that this all develops, or comes about in my daily life?"

I AM GLAD TO GIVE YOU several examples.

Remember that you have done what it says to do in Phase One. Also, Phase Two and Phase Three. Now, there is a "period of time" that it takes the seed to germinate and the harvest to arrive in the form of your dream fulfilled. This all takes place quite naturally from day to day in your life. But each day you will have ideas come into your mind and you will do what these ideas suggest as they have to do with the progress toward the attainment of your desires.

For example, suppose that you want to enjoy the standard of living which requires an income of one thousand dollars per month. But right now, your income is only three hundred seventy-five dollars per month.

Phase One, you identify your desire of an income of one thousand dollars per month.

Phase Two, you pretend and feel as you think you would feel if you already had an income of a thousand per month.

Phase Three, you would insist on maintaining that feeling regardless of any suggestion which would disagree with you.

Phase Four, you would listen for an idea from your subconscious mind which will help you to actually earn and receive the thousand per month. One day, you ask a friend of yours, "How many ways are there in the world, which pay at least a thousand per month income?"

He tells you of over one hundred ways that pay at least that much. Your Subconscious Mind begins to function in a manner that it never has before. It begins to add things up for you. It tells you in the form of ideas, out of the "blue" and in the form of feelings and urges that you should begin to study in a certain field, perhaps attend a series of lectures, or read certain books, or attain the necessary training to qualify for this new method which will permit you to earn and receive at least a thousand dollars per month. Of course, you not only listen to the subconscious, you do what it tells you to do.

You then, one day, find yourself in a new position that you enjoy very much and you are happier than you have ever been in your life. You are earning and receiving a thousand per month and your dream is a reality. The Count to Four Technique has worked for you and made it possible for you to almost triple your standard of living. It will help *THE WAY TO STATE* you to be anything you want to be and have anything you want to have.

Another example: A friend of mine is a man who, prior to three years ago, had never been in the direct selling field. He had been operating a modest dry cleaning business.

When I met him three years ago, he was a presser in a department store earning and receiving exactly $100 per week. He had never been before a group to make a talk at the time I met him. He had a 10th grade education, but like so many of us had not learned how to use the best of grammar as far as so-called correct speech was concerned. This man attended one of my lectures about three years ago, and he decided to do everything I asked him to do as I promised that he could be anything he wanted to be and that he could have anything he wanted to have.

In just three short years, he is a top sales executive of one of the most outstanding sales organizations in the world. His duties take him on lecture tours all over the United States, Canada, Hawaii and Alaska and soon he will go to Europe, Asia, Australia, New Zealand and Africa. He interviews the biggest people wherever he goes and his income is very substantial and is going up each year. He has everything he could desire. He lives in the finest suites at the finest hotels all over the world. He can do anything he desires because he has self confidence and an adequate amount of money.

Another example: About two years ago, I was lecturing along this line to a group of about 60 people near Los Angeles. Most of this small group were middle aged and older women in the selling field. I told them about the principles behind The Count to Four Technique. It was, as some of them told me later, just too good to be true. They wanted to believe it, but just found it impossible.

I felt this feeling among these very fine woman and I stopped right there on the spot and used The Count to Four Technique to help me to help them believe. I got the answer on the spot. I asked if there was at least one lady present, who is never, at any time, even secretly considered the idea of owning and casually driving a late model Cadillac automobile.

A charming lady raised her hand. In fact, several raised their hands, but I picked this one out as an example. I also asked her if she had an expensive dress. She said no, but that she would like one since I mentioned that she can have anything she wanted. Also, she said she was living in an apartment, which was very modest, that cost her about $30 per month. She was driving a used compact car, which at the time was worth about three-hundred and seventy-five dollars. I think that you all can get the picture.

Now, I told the group that in six months or less, this lady would own and be driving a late model Cadillac, be wearing a new expensive knit dress, and would be living in a new and expensive apartment comparable to her new way of life. They all looked goggle-eyed at me as though to say, "Can this really be true or is he a fool?"

Not six months later, but just 5 and one-half weeks later, this lady had her late model Cadillac, her knit dress and her new apartment. And all that she did was use what I have asked you to do in The Count to Four Technique.

She got well long into the plan, and after a week or so her subconscious mind began asking, "How can I earn and receive more money, because now I am a Cadillac girl and not a second-hand compact car girl. I'm a knit dress girl now, and I am a girl who lives in a new expensive apartment with period furniture. I want to find a way so I can be of greater service to humanity so that I can receive more compensation so I can comfortably live by my new standard."

Well, this lady's self-confidence and her sales increased so that she jumped from where she was at the time of the first lecture, to where she was just 5 and one-half weeks later. That has been a little less than two years ago, and now, I still know this very nice lady and at this time she is looking at a brand-new Cadillac. By the way, along with all the things which I mentioned, she also grew in poise, self-confidence, charm, patience, love of service, generosity, and many other very desirable mental attributes.

Her income today is at least three times what it was two years ago. Her self-confidence is 10 times what it was two years ago, and all because she decided to let me experiment in her case. She did not know exactly how it was going to happen, but she had confidence in me and did just exactly what I asked her to do. You say, "Yeah, he tells us these things, but he doesn't give us their names and addresses." If all you need, to believe this enough to try it, is to be able to contact this lady and ask her if I am telling you the truth, I'll be happy to give you names and addresses.

THE WAY TO STATE THE Phase Four principle is this:

The size and color of your thoughts are *cause*. Your experiences are *effect*.

Each thought has size and color or quality and quantity. Your thought regarding income is cause. Your income is effect.

If you could go through some sort of mental exercise and thereby increase the quality and quantity of your thought, which is cause, soon the income, which is effect, would be increased accordingly.

The Count to Four Technique is a mental exercise, which expands our thoughts regarding our desires and the law of cause and effect brings our desires to pass.

You ask Mr. A. how much his income is at present, and he tells you that it is $400 per month. You ask him what kind of a house he lives in, and he tells you he lives in a $75 per month house. You ask him why he doesn't live in a $200 per month house, on a $400 per month income.

Let's assume that he wants, very much, to live in a certain house which he can obtain for $200 per month. Let's now further assume that he goes to night school and gets a new job, where his services are now worth $650 per month instead of $400 per month. Now he obtains the $200 per month house and lives in it.

How much does it cost him? We will all have to admit that all he did was to increase the quality and quantity of his "thoughts" and this resulted in his 40 hours per week being worth $650 per month instead of the $400 earned previously. So, it didn't cost him anything to move into the $200 per month house from the $75 per month house.

Please try to think this through until it really means something to you. I know men who used to work very hard for $400 per month.

They worked hard for over 40 hours per week. Now they have so increased the value of their services per hour, that they work fewer hours, expand less energy and they are earning and receiving $4000 per month. I can take any man or woman, regardless of station in life, and if they will follow The Count to Four Technique, they can increase the quality and quantity of their "thoughts" and thereby increase the value of their services.

In turn, they will increase the amount of their income, and they can then obtain what they want. The Count to Four Technique will work for you regardless of whether your present income is $20 per week or $2000 per week. It is a principle which will make it possible for anyone, in any station in life, to merely decide what he wants to be and to have and then become it and have it.

It is now time that every person in the whole world should be told that success is just as simple as one, two, three, four. It is not as complicated as we have been told for centuries. It is good to get a formal education and to know as much as you can.

We have been told, however, that an education is indispensable and absolutely necessary before one can be successful. That is not so.

"If you can count to four", you can be anything you want to be and can have anything you want to have.

I know this to be true, and I challenge anyone to prove me wrong!

A Summary of The Science of Getting Rich

BY WALLACE D. WATTLES

First published 1910

THERE IS A THINKING STUFF FROM WHICH ALL THINGS ARE MADE, and which permeates, penetrates, and fills the inter-spaces of the universe.

A thought in this substance produces the thing that is imaged by the thought.

A person can form things in his thought, and by impressing your thought upon formless substance can cause the thing you think about to be created.

In order to do this, a person must pass from the competitive to the creative mind. Otherwise you cannot be in harmony with formless intelligence, which is always creative and never competitive in spirit.

A person may come into full harmony with the formless substance by entertaining a lively and sincere gratitude for the blessings it bestows upon you. Gratitude unifies your mind with the intelligence of substance, so that your thoughts are received by the formless. A person can remain upon the creative plane only by uniting yourself with the formless intelligence through a deep and continuous feeling of gratitude.

A person must form a clear and definite mental image of the things you wish to have, to do, or to become, and you must hold this mental image in your thoughts, while being deeply grateful that all your desires are granted to you. The person who wishes to get rich must spend your leisure hours in contemplating your vision, and in earnest thanksgiving that the reality is being given to you. Too much stress cannot be laid on the importance of frequent contemplation of the mental image, coupled with unwavering faith and devout gratitude. This is the process by which the impression is given to the formless and the creative forces set in motion.

The creative energy works through the established channels of natural growth, and of the industrial and social order. All that is included in your mental image will surely be brought to the person who follows the instructions given above, and whose faith does not waver. What you want will come to you through the ways of established trade and commerce.

In order to receive your own when it is ready to come to you, a person must be in action in a way that causes you to more than fill your present place. You must keep in mind the purpose to get rich through realization of your mental image. And you must do, every day, all that can be done that day, taking care to do each act in a successful manner. You must give to every person a use value in excess of the cash value you receive, so that each transaction makes for more life, and you must hold the advancing thought so that the impression of increase will be communicated to all with whom you come into contact.

The men and women who practice the foregoing instructions will certainly get rich, and the riches they receive will be in exact proportion to the definiteness of their vision, the fixity of their purpose, the steadiness of their faith, and the depth of their gratitude.

PMA: Science of Success – An Overview

IF YOU KNEW THE PATH to success, that it was already defined, and always worked if you just took those steps, would you let anything get in your way?

And if someone told you that you probably already knew most of what made the most successful that way, would you believe them?

The answer to those two different questions might be "no".

Because that's the way we've been trained from childhood - through our schools, our family upbringing, and the people around us, including our popular media.

We aren't trained to be an exceptional success – instead, we're trained to get a job and stick with it as long as we can.

Whether you work at a writer or in any other profession or job – your success is based on a set of natural principles.

And most of us have already encountered some or all of them through just regular living.

The only difference between the exceptional successes and the ordinary mundane job-holder is a matter of belief and persistence.

If you don't believe that success is inevitable, then it doesn't make sense to go out of your way to achieve it. It's much easier to just follow the crowd and do what they do.

That explains why the vast bulk of job-holders live from paycheck to paycheck, and get loans that last the bulk of their years in the workforce.

What if someone said that all you have to do is to think for yourself? That it's mostly a matter of believing your gut instincts are right?

This is the deal: *Success at anything in life is based on a set of natural principles that you are already familiar with.* You already know that these work for you. But the scene is that you have never worked out what they are exactly, why they are important, and how to line up your actions to make any repeatable success for yourself.

The real secret is to study successful people and find what the common principles are that they use. Of course, that would take a lifetime – so we are better off finding people who have already done this.

Napoleon Hill was probably the most influential speaker and author in the last century because that is what he did. He said Carnegie commissioned him to that challenge – to distill that practical philosophy of achievement. All we know for sure is that he did wind up with a set of principles. The proof is found in his "Think and Grow Rich" - a book that reportedly made more millionaires than any other single fiction or non-fiction book ever published (excepting, perhaps, the Bible).

People who read and internalize that book are different at the end. They become successful at almost anything they try to do. One reason is because they focus on one goal and persist at achieving it until they do.

IN THAT LAST SENTENCE are three of the principles. Can you spot them?

Goal.

Focus.

Persistence.

And you might say, it can't be that simple. I'd have to agree with you. Because Hill, late in his life, and after spending almost all of that life in distilling the Philosophy of Personal Achievement – had to be talked out of retirement to put a final polish on these 17 natural success principles.

What I'm about to show you, briefly, is a short explanation of each one and a way you can learn and remember all of these. Just so you can now start your studies of these principles while you get busy becoming even *more* successful – at *anything* you want to be successful in.

Whatever you want to be. Whatever you want to achieve, attain, or acquire.

Because if you're reading this, you've already been successful at many things. Like learning to read, for instance. Or learning to dress yourself and hold a job in order to earn income so you could buy this book - or at least find it in the library. Maybe it was learning how to research and find things online.

The point of life - and this book - is to learn how to become as successful as you really want, at anything and everything you could possibly want. Because nothing is really holding you back except what limits you've accepted and still hold in your own mind.

You can really get everything you want out of life. And keep it.

Napoleon Hill started from scratch and made himself a millionaire three separate times in his life. Others, like W. Clement Stone turned a hundred dollars into 10 million by following what Hill worked out.

Earl Nightingale was exceptionally successful at almost everything he tried - and left us around 9,000 recordings of tips and tricks to living. Again, only after he found and started applying Hill's book.

You can find modern, contemporary examples of this - any search engine will give you names of the rich and famous who have digested Hill's books and lectures.

Your own next question is, perhaps, so why aren't I successful? How come I don't have everything I want out of life?

And looking for that answer is probably the reason you are reading this book, or listening to this audio, or watching this video.

While you are going to have to answer that particular question for yourself, I can give you a broad hint:

You don't believe that you already know how.

This short book is here to expose you to these natural principles, in a particular order, and help you orient your efforts around them to get just as successful as you want.

I'm going to present these principles in a format where you can remember them simply. And tell you a bit about how they work. However, this is a only very brief introduction. It's going to be up to you to research and test these in your own life – to prove or disprove them for yourself.

THERE ARE FIVE MAIN subject areas to learn. You can count them off on five of your fingers:

1. Goal Achievement,
2. Focused Thinking,

3. A Positive Mindset,
4. Creative Problem-solving, and
5. A Balanced Lifestyle.

Within these areas are a total of 17 principles. This model was developed so you can keep all these principles in mind. The reason for this is that all these 17 principles form a system. And they interact and build on each other as you learn them. Being able to identify each principle in action will help you test them for yourself.

Once you've gone through these simple introductory essays, then your testing can take a more intense approach. Because you'll now know the definitions of these principles and you'll start seeing them show up all through your everyday life. And you'll see where you can prove them through testing on a daily basis.

Until you prove them to yourself, through your own testing, you won't believe anyone who claims they do work. And that is a healthy skepticism. When you have tested them for yourself, then you can decide.

The difference between disbelief and belief is a single decision. And the difference between success and failure is often just a single thought. But you can change your mind and change your thoughts if you want to. It's all up to you.

THE POINT OF BECOMING a successful writer is to start by defining your purpose and to know the success system to follow that will lead you to your ultimate success.

If you want to become a successful writer, you have to study success. And this is most easily done by studying people who have already studied success and written up what they found so others could follow.

These essays show you that simple path, briefly laid out for you. All who have studied, tested, and applied the materials that follow become successful. If they met with temporary failure, they then turned that around to make their success even greater.

What you're about to read lays out a challenging adventure ahead.

So, let's get started.

I. Goal Achievement

IN THIS FIRST AREA, this subject breaks down into three principles:

- Definite Purpose,

- Applied Faith (Persistence),

- Master Mind.

The very simple first step toward becoming a success is to decide exactly what it is that you want most out of life.

This is taking the action of defining your purpose. A purpose is another name for a goal.

Goals consist of what you want to *be* in life. They are also a concise statement of what you want to *have* in life.

So you define your purpose.

Hill laid out six steps for this:

1. Write down exactly what you want out of life. It's whatever success seems to be for you.

2. Work out what you want to give in order to exchange for that success. Write that down, too.

3. Establish a definite date by when you intend to possess the desired thing.

4. Create a definite plan for carrying out your desire and begin at once, whether you feel entirely ready or not, to put this plan into action.

5. Write out a clear, concise statement of your responses to the preceding four steps.

6. Read your written statement aloud at least twice daily. Once after arising in the morning and once just before retiring at night. As you read, see and feel and believe yourself already in possession of whatever your goal happens to be.

As you devote yourself and your energies to achieving this goal, you'll find certain "coincidences" showing up in your life.

These will happen to the same degree you have faith in yourself and your ability to achieve whatever it is that you want most out of life.

Faith is another word for persistence. So as you persist in devoting everything you can to achieving this goal, the more it will start appearing for you. These "coincidences" probably have always been there, but now you are looking for them and they seem to just "show up".

But your faith has to be *applied*. You have to turn your daily actions into those that will accomplish your plan. You have to persist.

Now, your plan will need revision or streamlining from time to time. So: revise it when you need to, and get started implementing the new version immediately.

Again, you're reading your goal statement out loud several times each and every day. So this helps you stay focused on that defined purpose you've laid out.

The third part of this first area is to look for people you can form a "Master Mind Alliance" with. Such an alliance is when you and another person share information and suggestions on how to improve your progress toward a goal. It's not a social group. The people who you go into this alliance with don't have to know your whole plan, nor do they have to agree with all you do. They do agree with some specific part of it and can be consulted with just that part.

In that specific area they are in agreement with you and completely supportive. You can get with them and review your progress in that area. They will give you ideas to speed that progress or actions that will streamline your work. Or they will simply be a kind, open ear - and give you the "atta-boy" and encouragement you need. Hill's suggestion is to find someone in your immediate family and someone who is benefiting from your executing your plan.

For Henry Ford, this was his wife. There had never been a self-propelled automobile before, and there were other tinkerers who were competing in the area. Ford's wife simply kept him fired up about his purpose, encouraged him to pursue his dream..

Later in life, Ford was said to have a row of buttons on his desk. Each one went to ring someone in some area of his business to do with automobile manufacturing. He had an expert in each area he could consult with.

Steel magnate Andrew Carnegie was said to know little about the steel industry itself. But he had a small army of executives over the various areas who did. And so he led them to success by consulting their knowledge to achieve his own broad purpose.

Do these steps above - get your definite purpose written down, along with what you'll give to get it, and read this out loud several times daily.

Work out your plan, then work your plan – and persist in making it work. That's "Applied Faith" in action.

Form a Master Mind Alliance with someone inside your family and also someone outside it to help you accomplish that purpose.

Just applying these first three principles will get you firmly started on your own road to success.

II. Focused Thinking

THIS AREA CONSISTS of:

- Accurate Thinking,

- Focused Attention,

- Self-Discipline.

We each have something like 60,000 thoughts per day. And most people have never learned to focus their attention and thinking to accomplish anything from all those thoughts.

In fact, many people simply pick up books and movies to read and watch just so they can get distracted from their thoughts.

Meanwhile, the increasing speed and access to data has made a problem of choosing what we should think about. "News" is often non-factual at best. And free advice is worth exactly what you pay for it.

Your thinking has to be accurate.

To improve your accuracy, you have to be able to determine facts.

A fact is something that can be observed in the physical universe. You don't have to do the observing, but someone has to vouch that it occurred.

You should be able to ask someone where they got that data from - did they or the person who told them actually see it happen?

Supposition or hearsay is useless. If you can't verify what someone tells you is based on facts, then it won't help you achieve your goal. Discard any useless data. Stick to the verified facts that work for you.

The other type of possibly useful thinking can be in the form of conclusions based on reasoning.

Reasoning has two types - *Inductive reasoning*: where you take two factual datums and predict into the future that a third fact exists or will exist out there. *Deductive reasoning* is almost the reverse: if this fact was the result, and there was an earlier change that occurred before it, then there should be yet another action or circumstance that helped cause that result.

Both reasonings do not themselves prove a fact exists - only that it's *probable* that a fact does exist, if you look for and verify it.

Conclusions based on facts will be useful to you only if they are based on verified facts. Opinions, no matter who gives them, are only as useful as they are based on facts. Free opinions are usually worth just what you pay for them.

Not all the facts that you find will be useful. The important facts you find will help you achieve your goal. So that also narrows down the sources you should pay attention to.

All that is part of Accurate Thinking. You are winnowing down to the important facts you can use. Winnowing down to individual sources who routinely provide fact-based reports.

Meanwhile, you are also improving your focus. Your attention needs to be invested into tracking what will help you achieve your goal.

It's that simple. The more focused you are onto achieving, acquiring, or attaining your goal, the sooner it will start showing up for you. Having attention on several other dis-related areas may distract you from getting anything done towards your definite purpose.

Being able to focus narrowly on your chosen purpose requires self-discipline. And that improves your ability to guide and control your own thoughts, which then helps you achieve whatever it is that you want most out of life.

People who have not been trained in self-discipline tend to drift in life. As drifters, they find one day that most of their life is over and they have little to show for it. The "alpha's" you may have heard about are simply those who have a definite purpose and have narrowed their focus and and honed their thinking and actions to achieving that one goal.

Simple. Focusing your thinking and attention requires some self-discipline, but are much more rewarding than just drifting.

III. A Positive Mindset

THIS AREA INCLUDES the principles of:

- Pleasing Personality,

- Positive Mental Attitude,

- Enthusiasm,

- Personal Initiative, and

- Going the Extra Mile.

A mindset is composed of habitual thinking patterns. While you are trained by family and your environment from the day you are born (and sometimes, even pre-natally) - this training can be examined and re-programmed. Any mental habit you have can be can be tweaked or replaced to help you achieve whatever you want out of life.

Emotions are pre-programmed responses to external stimulus. The etymological roots of this word means literally "motion out". You use an emotion to cope with inputs from your environment.

Feelings are more perceptions of how things are. While you can *feel* happy, you can *emote* enthusiasm. While you can *feel* sad, you can *emote* grief and depression.

While feelings and emotions are often interchanged as words, it can't be understated how diffrent these two are. Confusing these two enables people to become the effect of their overwrought emotions. They tend to live these emotions instead of simply observing the feeling for what it is, letting it go, and then moving back to getting that purpose achieved.

There are whole books written on nothing but developing a positive mental attitude, but here we just want to touch on the high points.

A simple mental habit is one most of us already have - when you greet someone, it's with an honest smile and grace.

The next is to find out how they are doing that day, that moment. Be honestly interested in how their day is going so far.

Hesitate in telling them anything about your own day unless you are asked.

Again, you can't get anything unless you give first. If you want cooperation from someone else, the best thing to do is to listen to them first and see if there is anything you can do to help them with whatever they are experiencing that day.

Now, in the conversation that develops, of course you acknowledge what they tell you, which just lets them know you are honestly interested in what they have to say.

A positive attitude is denoted by the tone of your voice, your facial expression, your courtesy and consideration you show. A negative attitude will show them what you think of them, almost by telepathy.

A few other traits we have space to tell you here: you should be flexible in all situations to adjust without losing your composure or becoming irritable or angry. It's controlling your unwanted reaction (emotion) that self-discipline enables.

Another trait is your ability to show enthusiasm toward that person. Enthusiasm you must train, like any other emotion, to turn on and off at will - to exhibit it when it's appropriate. It will attract like a magnet, bringing many people toward you, as this is rarely exhibited by most in our culture. So you want to invest it only on people you want to support, and so - support your works.

The last trait we'll cover here is your sincerity of purpose. This cannot be faked. Be honest with yourself and develop this integrity with others as well. People will quickly find out, distrust, and distance themselves from a fake. Be real at all times.

All this is a matter of manners. And manners are simply how you'd like to be treated. That's how you treat others. Just good manners.

So you develop a sense of how much conversation the other person wants to share. Many people have no one to actually listen to them, and no outlet for their observations about life. Good listeners are in short supply.

You don't need criticism and carping in your life, and so learn how to extract yourself from listening to gossip. None of that will forward your goal. So minimize your time with such people.

Seek to understand people before offering your own opinions, however valid the facts or reasoning. Those ideas won't probably be shared at first. And try to give only positive and creative approaches that they might be able to put to use - but only if they want to hear it. Often, just listening to someone is the best way to help them.

Again, the conversation should be about what you can do for them. And if it's obvious that this person will not be able to help you in any way with your goal, then extract yourself as best you can. You do have to help others with their goals before you can enable them to help you with yours. But 98% of everyone out there has no real goal for their lives. And a largish proportion of these are simply critical of everyone, which extends internally to themselves. Critical people seek to tear down anything and anyone they get involved with. That's their mental mindset. Avoid.

Still, if you are routinely pleasant to everyone you meet, regardless of how they treat you, you'll be training them to be pleasant in return.

Try to treat everyone as an equal. People who dominate the discussion all the time, and order others around also have that problem in their own life - it's out of control to them. And you won't be able to help them much with any suggestion. Still, you can lend an ear for a bit of time at least.

You're looking for people open to supporting you in return, just as you've supported others by respecting them.

———————

ANOTHER POINT OF RESPECTING others is to dress well, stand up straight. It also builds your own esteem. Practice makes perfect. A self-confident person will tend to build other's self-confidence through their actions.

One idea to get started in this is to use W. Clement Stone's affirmation, "I feel healthy, I feel happy, I feel terrific!" This will often put a smile on your face just by itself. And smiling then brings the rest of your physical being into that attitude. Stone lived to be a hundred years old. So saying this, even if under your breath in a crowd, can work wonders for your attitude - regardless of the day you've had so far.

What we've also touched on here is personal initiative.

This, too, is a broader subject Hill studied and wrote about. The key point is that your purpose should be big enough, interesting enough, and personal enough that you can devote all your energies directly toward its achievement.

Your plan is worked out. So you work that plan by taking initiative to execute those steps you know have to be done. The old phrase tells you how much initiative you are going to need - "A winner never quits and a quitter never wins." So we see our Applied Faith principle coming back to visit us again.

The end of your day should conclude with writing out a short list of the six most important things you must get done the next day. Put that list in your pocket.

Just before you go to sleep, meditate on what you accomplished that day and what you plan to accomplish the next day. Envision yourself as also accomplishing these next steps successfully.

When you wake, you'll often have inspiration on how to deal with them, or be more efficient at them. Then, when you are back at work, pull out that list and work on the most important one on that list - it should be at the top. Work on only that first step until it gets done successfully. Then start and complete the next item on your list until all six are successfully completed.

This is great practice in self-initiative, and also setting sub-goals.

We can now discuss Going the Extra Mile principle, since we've already mentioned the Golden Rule above.

Render more and better service than that for which you are paid, and sooner or later you will receive compound interest on compound interest from your investment.

It's inevitable that every seed of useful service you sow will multiply itself and come back to you in overwhelming abundance.

If you do this, you'll be rewarded in several definite ways. You will sooner or later receive compensation far exceeding the actual value of the service you render. You will exhibit greater strength of character. You will find it easier to maintain a positive mental attitude at all times. You will find that there is a permanent market for your services. And you will experience the thrill of new and stronger convictions of courage and self-reliance, new surges of the self-starting power of personal initiative, and an energizing influx of vital enthusiasm.

It's simple - you can't get without giving. If you give extra beyond what is required, then the Universe eventually has to return and balance itself. Your job is simply to keep the lines open so that the return can flow (or flood) back to you.

That's the point of this section. Your mental attitude sets the stage for all manner of things. But you keep it aligned to your definite purpose so you don't waste any energy.

There's the reason for this Science of Success course, through these short introductory essays. As you master and continue to improve your mastery of these 17 natural principles, the wealth and abundance that you will earn all starts with your giving in excess from the first minute you start driving toward your goal.

IV. Creative Problem-Solving

THIS AREA HAS TWO PRINCIPLES:

- Creative Vision,

- Learning From Adversity,

There's an additional benefit to having a definite purpose and focusing your thoughts and efforts on that one thing.

Your imagination starts bringing you solutions to any number of problems you encounter.

Of course, it doesn't start right off, but as you continue to read your written goal statement daily, it trains your imagination to find and propose those answers for you.

How does that work?

There are three minds at work. Your *Conscious* mind is the one you can control directly. The *Infinite* mind has all knowledge, all answers - but you cannot access it. Between these two is your *Subconscious* or *Unconscious* mind. The Unconscious mind is always there, always present. And it acts as the bridge between your Conscious mind and all the answers you could possibly need.

You can get what you want through insistent and persistent repetition to your Unconscious of exactly what it is that you need help with. Take time daily to read and repeat your goal out loud. Use any spare moment to envision that end result appearing all around you. Feel the feelings you will have when it occurs. Really get that feeling of delight and satisfaction in your mind.

Your Unconscious mind will pick up on that concept and its feelings, and then pass it along, with all the other questions you have, to the Infinite Mind - and then bring back the answers.

Now, the clarity of that answer will depend on how clearly you state your request. So it takes a bit of practice to learn how to get your needs and wants across. Again, these have to be in alignment to your major goal – that one you've written down.

This is your own personal creative resource – your bottomless well of inspired thought. As you master this, you can come up with all the answers you could possibly need.

Life isn't always perfect. Sometimes the worst catastrophes can loom large in front of us. Any and every problem, whether overwhelming or minor, has an opportunity for success at its core. Take apart that disastrous occurrence and see what you can extract from it as a potential solution, a way out.

Then apply what you have discovered and turn that to your advantage. Many great men have lost their fortunes completely - and then built them right back, bigger than before. But only where they persisted, when they examined all their actions, and then re-impressed their mind with the concept and feelings of success at whatever they intend to achieve, acquire, or attain.

Because these two natural principles are exact and inexorable. They always work. You just have to put them to work.

V. A Balanced Lifestyle

THIS AREA HAS FOUR principles:

- Cooperation & Teamwork,

- Maintaining Sound Health,

- Budgeting Time and Money,

- Developing Your Natural Balance.

In the world around you, there are many people who want to help you. As part of any workforce, there are associates who want to do their job, just as much as you want to do yours. They will cooperate with you as part of any workforce. This is rudimentary teamwork.

Now, that cooperation can be grudging or hesitant, as well as positive and abundant. It depends on how well you have mastered your own mindset and encouraged others to master theirs.

When you develop positive teamwork at your job, or within your business, that work can become a labor of joy.

Teamwork isn't a true Master Mind scene. Anyone who has worked as a job where everyone did "only as much as they had to" can tell you that it's not always fun to come to work every day. Such a job isn't anything you look forward to. And why the weekends are such delights to escape to.

Where you can align everyone at your job or in your business to achieving the goal of that company, to fulfilling the purpose of their individual position within that business, the production moves smoothly and work can be a positive experience, where time just flies by and your shift is over almost too soon. You have lots of energy left over at the end of your work day and perhaps even a smile on your face from your satisfying working conditions and the good job you did that day.

Your cooperation and teamwork with others is a large part of living a balanced lifestyle.

Another key area to build your lifestyle around is maintaining your sound health.

While there are many advices and experts in this field, pay some attention to the basic trio of your diet, your sleep, and your exercise.

Eating too much of what isn't good for us can lead to poor health. Insufficient quality of sleep, and avoiding exercise can also allow your body to get run down.

Use of your body is a necessary requisite to whatever you are producing in life. You can even make it a small goal as part of your overall goal - just to keep your body in good shape and able to help you enjoy life all around you.

Throughout your lifetime, you'll also need to budget your time and money. While it's true that you can reinvest your money to get more back than you started with, each of us has a limited amount of time on this planet. And having insufficient funds to live life with can also take the joy out of living. So work these out for yourself and budget every thing you do and spend to get the most out of them.

And finally, look through your lifestyle for balance. Nature is built to keep all things in balance. Humans, with their various thought processes, consider that they can ignore the signs of imbalance in their lives. This arrogance itself is the cause of many failures.

Nature will always work to bring balance through your habits and those of people around you. As you push toward your goal, your positive mindset will help you help others improve their lives and own mindset. In that way, everyone wins.

But it all starts with you and your definite purpose.

And So...

AS YOU GO THROUGH YOUR life, you develop mental habits that will either help or hinder you in your progress. Through these short essays, you've already been told about several areas that you can improve, starting with defining your purpose. As you align your various habits to achieving that success you want, you will tweak or adjust the various habits you have to more closely approach what it is you really want out of life.

Always be prepared to make the large or small adjustments so that you can live in harmony with Nature's various cycles. And always be willing to go the extra mile to help others open-handedly as you travel your own success path.

By taking some time to regularly review these 17 principles of Napoleon Hill's Science of Success course, you will be able to live the life you've always dreamed of. You'll be able to attain, achieve, and acquire *everything* you've ever wanted from life. Then keep your gains – forever.

And the second best time to start – is *now*.

How to Keep What You Got

LESTER LEVENSON WAS sent home to die at the age of 42. He had been a success at nearly everything he tried. Brilliant, he earned a full scholarship and received several degrees. Turning his hand to manufacturing, mining, and sales, all his businesses usually turned out successful as long as he was running them directly.

Yet, his health continued to worsen, almost to spite all his success. Chronic migraines, perforated ulcers, and major coronaries (heart attacks) – these finally led his doctor to tell him to simply go home and rest. With the medicine at that time, he was told that *any* physical effort could be his last.

So he was left with only his mind to work things out. Throwing away all that he had studied in school, he started simply analyzing himself from the inside out. In three months, he worked out what was bothering him and incidentally solved his health problems as well.

What he discovered left him in such a high state that it took over eighteen years of intense research after that, studying all manner of religious and philosophical texts, just to understand what he had achieved.

For our use, his work boils down to some very basic rules:

a. The basic purpose all of us have in this existence – is to survive through a human body, as an individual.

b. This can be stated as simply four desires:

- The need or want for *security*.

- The need or want for *approval*.

- The need or want for *control,* or to escape control.

- The need to *belong.*

c. These mental habits we have amassed are the one flaw in all these books and lessons on goal achievement.

It's not that you can't get anything and everything you want.

But keeping those results from there on out is another thing entirely.

Those four desires might be part of the reason for you achieving your goal. But they can also be the very reasons you can lose whatever you've achieved.

Here's the secret to keeping everything you've gained:

Treat others <u>only</u> as you would want to be treated.

To get and keep everything you ever wanted out of life, you simply need to work for the best of all concerned. The greater numbers of humanity – and all life forms on this planet – that you include in your goals, the more assistance you will attract to help you achieve them.

And you need to help people find what you know about achieving goals. You should share what you know about attaining success open-handedly.

Like the way you've been treated through this book.

d. The reasons you wouldn't keep everything you've earned are due to succumbing to those emotional desires above.

Giving into those desires is what makes you treat others poorly. Not the way you'd like to be treated.

And so, a downward spiral starts of bad decisions to justify what you just did. Very similar to the Sir Walter Scott quote: "What a tangled web we weave, when first we practice to deceive."

For these four emotional desires are lies at their base. You generate all your own emotions as reactions to the world around you. The word "emotion" actually means "to send out."

Compassion is a feeling, like openhanded help. Feelings are personal, internal, honest. Hate and anger are emotions – they go out. Happy is a feeling – it's inside. You show it with a smile, or a hug.

Almost all emotions, if not all, have been trained in by your living, your schooling, the movies you've watched. All those drama's. Those four desires are emotional, and can be let go.

And when you let them go, you can get a great deal of your sanity back. Above all, you'll make the decisions that will help you give better value to all concerned. So you not only keep whatever you've always wanted to get out of life – it will expand and expand.

e. Release negative emotions to keep what you have as long as you want them.

Now, those habitual desires can be removed with simple releasing.

Releasing is simply a few steps:

1. Finding what desire is present at that moment.
2. Recognizing it.
3. Deciding to let it go.
4. And then letting it go.

It's far too simple.

- You see you're upset by something.

- Pause. Take a breath to relax. Ask yourself which of those four desires are present (or in what combination). Acknowledge their presence. Decide you can let them go. Then do so.

- If they're still here, you can repeat those steps. Or not.

The point is that you won't make a bad emotional decision just because one of your trained-in emotions have been triggered.

You already know how to get everything you want out of life.

And if you do these two steps consistently:

1. Do only actions which help the majority – as you'd like to be treated (not selfishly or being greedy).
2. And keeping yourself on a positive footing by releasing your negative emotions.

Then you'll be able to get and keep anything and everything you want out of life.

Any fears to the contrary, met with courage, will be found to be false – and eventually quit bothering you.

———————

HOW NAPOLEON HILL EARNED and lost his millionaire fortune – *twice*.

You'll have to search for this, but you'll find that Hill was a millionaire before the Great Depression, with a fleet of Rolls-Royce's and a large rural estate in New York. All earned with proceeds from his first bestselling 7-volume book and course, "Law of Success".

Then he lost it all.

He became a millionaire again after writing and releasing his "Think and Grow Rich".

But lost that as well – even the rights to that bestselling book.

Late in life, he earned his third millionaire-level income – and kept it. Actually, his third wife managed his last fortune, and wisely set up a Foundation to take care of his intellectual properties.

And that Foundation watches over his trademarks today.

For all the spiritual principles that Hill has in his books, he missed something. (And you can see where he learned that lesson in his last book, "Get Rich Through Peace of Mind", published four years before his death.)

Hill studied and distilled a set of common-sense success principles. And telling others about them made him rich. Three times.

What he didn't understand, until his last few years, was how to spot and deal with the booby traps of unwanted human emotion that can bring down everything you've built up. Otherwise, those unwanted and unnecessary emotions just keep on wrecking your life.

Napoleon Hill tested and refined all he studied from the people he met through his own life. And studying Hill's own life gives us even more examples of how to successfully manage our own.

WITHIN THIS BOOK ARE the keys to resolving any reason you can't have and keep anything you want out of life.

And if you don't feel you need all that stuff after enjoying it for awhile – you can simply release it and let it go.

There are four questions you might ask yourself about the things you want – and the things you have:

- Does this make my life *simpler*?

- Does this help me live in greater *peace* with myself and others?

- Does this bring more *joy* into my life?

- And finally, does this help me manifest *abundance*?

———————

WHILE IT IS TRUE THAT you can't take it all with you, some mystics say that our time here may be only a step in a longer journey, that death is simply a doorway to another experience. And what we improve in ourselves is never truly lost when you step through.

If you can use this time, right here and now, to seek such elements you find in this existence – ones that bring you continuing simple, joyful, inner peace – might that understanding be worth everything?

The 7 Simple Steps to Releasing for Personal Development

(EXCERPTED AND EXTRACTED from the tape series "The Way" these notes describe a very direct manner of re-achieving your personal Freedom. And whether you're looking for life's abundance or how to get rich – it's all in these 7 simple steps of Levenson releasing technique...)

The steps:

1. Want Freedom more than you want the World.

2. Take all your joy from within by releasing.

3. Make the decision to go Free and then do it.

4. Go directly to the fear of dying and then release it.

5. Get everything from here on by direct releasing.

6. Be not the doer. Be the witness. Let go and let God.

7. Make your behavior that which a Master would do.

Once you decide to get moving on the path to total freedom, you will eventually make it out. The only reason these materials exist is to enable you to do it in a single lifetime, this one.

All the joy there is in life already exists within you. You just have to release all the limitations that you hold in place to keep this from showing up.

You set up the decision to go Free and just work at it. Don't resist anything, just push this right on up and you'll make it. Keep striving for this and you'll arrive. The more you concentrate on it, the faster it shows up.

All the other points – control, approval, security are all based on the fear of dying. Simply go to the central fear of dying – release it directly and completely – and the rest falls away. You have to quit trying to make the body survive – to exist through the body. (But it's suggested by several releasing technique counselors that you spend significant time releasing before you try this on your own – it has at times made people physically sick.)

There's nothing you want that can't be more easily and rapidly acquired (it will show up faster) if you just release on the fact of it's being there now. Look for anything that comes up when you accept the goal of that product or service being present right now in your life.

Don't effort at doing anything. Flow with the actions around you. You'll get intuitive insight on what actions you should be doing. Just be the witness to what is going on. You'll see the actions happening around you and you only just have to move with what you should do to achieve harmony in your own life and the world around you. Just let go of any effort and let the God in you do the doing that makes sense in the moment.

Act only in ways as a Master would. The more you just follow the Master presence which is already within you, the more will show up on the external "you" which everyone else then sees. You will then start intuitively to do the right actions, the necessary actions, the harmonious actions. And all things that you actually want in life will show up for you. What you want will change. What you want now isn't necessarily what you are going to wind up with – it will be a lot better, a lot bigger, far more of it than you want or think you want right now. Just get off the thinking and act only as a Master would. And let it show up around you.

Welcoming

(FROM "THE GREATEST Secret" by Rhonda Byrne)

The brilliant teacher and ex-physicist Francis Lucille describes one method of releasing negative feelings as "welcoming." Welcoming has proven to be one of the most powerful practices I have ever done in my life. This practice eradicates negative feelings once and for all.

(It's also worth noting that the situation or circumstance that caused the negative feeling in the first place will also change when you welcome the negative feeling. This is due to you releasing the feeling you have about the situation.)

Welcoming is the opposite of resisting. Resistance says to a negative feeling, "No, I don't want this!" And welcoming says, "Yes, you are welcome here." Awareness is always welcoming of everything. No negative feeling, no matter how strong, can stand up against the welcoming of Awareness. In fact, no negativity whatsoever can stand up against the welcoming of Awareness.

It seems counterintuitive to welcome something you don't want, but it's resistance that holds what you don't want to you, and welcoming stops you from resisting! It can be challenging not to resist or tense up against a negative feeling, but when you open your attention and welcome the feeling, miraculously the resistance ceases, and the negative feeling—which is just energy—dissolves. The situation that you were resisting will then be able to change.

Remember, opening your attention is like zooming out with a camera lens so you're not focused on any detail with your mind. Make sure that you don't focus into the feeling. That will make it stronger, because the mind increases anything we focus on. Notice the feeling, but don't focus into it. Keep your attention wide.

Teacher Hale Dwoskin suggests that, in the beginning, it can be helpful to open your arms out to the side of your body when you open your attention. Open your arms as though you are welcoming somebody you love whom you're about to embrace. This helps you open your heart (we have a tendency to keep the heart area of our body permanently contracted, without realizing we're doing it). I consciously open my heart when I welcome anything in life that I do not want.

My teacher says that when we're welcoming, we are being our true self, Awareness, because welcoming is our very nature. In fact, the Infinite Awareness that you are is so welcoming that negative feelings can't possibly remain in its presence. Quite simply, when you welcome anything negative, you allow it to dissolve back into its source—You, Awareness! And so when you welcome a negative feeling you are tapping into your infinite power to dissolve it.

Teacher Francis Lucille says that as we become more established in welcoming, we realize that welcoming is not really an activity of its own; rather, welcoming stops the activity of resistance. Initially we think that welcoming is something we do, and as we practice it more, we realize that it's actually stopping us from doing something many of us do automatically—resisting.

The Super Practice

THIS IS A SIMPLE BUT powerful combination of the two most important and vital practices in this book—welcoming and staying as Awareness.

Step 1. Welcome Anything Negative

Open your heart and welcome any negative reactions, negative feelings, negative sensations, negative thoughts or problems, in the moment they appear.

Step 2. Stay as Awareness

Stay as Awareness by keeping your attention wide like the lens on a camera, so it's not focused on any detail.

Because Awareness is naturally welcoming, you will find after doing the Super Practice for a while that the two steps merge into one. In the moment you welcome, you'll find that Awareness is instantaneously present.

YOUR WORLD IS FILLED WITH STRANGE SECRETS

...that are hidden in plain sight.

THEY ARE STRANGE BECAUSE they are commonly known in our literature and history.

Solutions to poverty, lack, disappointment.

And people who discover them think they are the first to figure them out.

There are tons of books out there that essentially say the same thing. *And have existed through all our long written history and literature.*

This is what Earl Nightingale found when he wrote and recorded his 78RPM LP record in *1957*. And it was such a breakthrough that it became the first Gold record of its kind - *all without any advertising.*

*Because he struck a common chord that explains **all** success.*

It's time for you to get everything you want out of life.

Let me give you a small book that tells you exactly how this works.

To help you, I've taken Nightingale's original recording and made its transcript available for you, along with short versions of the books he recommends on that recording. Plus some other related essays and articles. All slim enough to fit on your smartphone or ereader for ready review - anywhere, any time.

All at no-charge, no cost.

It doesn't cost you even a penny to kickstart your success.

To get what you want. Everything you want.

Limited Time Offer

You can download your own copy of this book – as long as still available.

*Visit: [1]**https://calm.li/SSC-NF***

---

1. *https://calm.li/SSC-NF*

RECOMMENDED BOOKS YOU MAY LIKE

ALL OUR LATEST RELEASES[1]

Both fiction and non-fiction – each with links to major online book outlets as well as author discounts.

The Strangest Secret Library[2]

All the full references mentioned in Earl Nightingale's Strangest Secret Library available for instant download – through your online book outlet of choice or with our publisher's discount.

Books on Success and Goal Achievement[3]

Our collection of modern and classic references on how you can become a personal success and achieve your own goals – to get *everything* you want out of life.

Books on Writing & [4]Publishing[5]

---

1. https://livesensical.com/
   books/?utm_campaign=related-book-ad&utm_source=ebook

2. https://livesensical.com/book-series/
   strangest-secret-library/?utm_campaign=related-book-ad&utm_source=ebook

3. https://livesensical.com/book-series/how-to-completely-change-your-life/

4. https://livesensical.com/book-series/
   publishing-and-writing/?utm_campaign=related-book-ad&utm_source=ebook

5. https://livesensical.com/book-series/
   publishing-and-writing/?utm_campaign=related-book-ad&utm_source=ebook

Our collection of modern and classic references on how to improve your writing in our modern self-publishing age.

Speculative F[6]iction [7]Modern Parables[8]

Our short stories and anthologies – all in order of most recent release.

Classic Fiction[9]

Our ever-expanding collection of fiction stories that are hard to find, yet their stories never grow old. Perfect entertainment when the too-modern world becomes stale...

———————————

Visit https://livesensical.com/go/find-your-book/ to find the book you're looking for

6. https://livesensical.com/book-series/

   fiction/?utm_campaign=related-book-ad&utm_source=ebook

7. https://livesensical.com/book-series/

   fiction/?utm_campaign=related-book-ad&utm_source=ebook

8. https://livesensical.com/book-series/

   fiction/?utm_campaign=related-book-ad&utm_source=ebook

9. https://livesensical.com/book-series/fiction-classics/

COURSES TO EXPAND UNDERSTANDING

AS TIME AND RESOURCES become available, our ongoing plans include expanding this library of references into interactive courses, such as:

The Strangest Secret

Based on the classic Gold Record, this course enables you to more carefully study and apply the wisdom Earl Nightingale recorded for all humankind to improve their lives with.

If You Can Count to Four

The test of all Dr. J. B. Jones had studied about goal achievement and success led to an eight figure income and national corporation within five years. This course is based on his bestseller that defined his philosophy of achievement.

Get Everything You Want out of Life

Jones' vice president was known as the "Millionaire Maker" because he used his mentor's process. His one surviving recording gives a unique approach to the idea of being anything you want to be and having anything you want to have.

PMA: Science of Success – An Overview

Napoleon Hill was persuaded to come out of retirement and do a final polish on his Practical Philosophy of Achievement. This course gives an overall view and mnemonics to learn the 17 natural principles he discovered.

Think Less and Grow Richer

Once you have everything you want, you'll come to the realization that nothing you can buy will keep you happy all the time. This book is the bridge from goal achievement right on up to permanent high levels of personal esteem – all regardless of how your world treats you.

And more under development...

All based on classic texts from this collected library that remain unknown by modern "guru's".

Visit https://livesensical.com/go/goal-achievement-courses/
for latest developments

RELATED BOOKS OF INTEREST

———

HERE ARE SEVERAL BOOKS published by Midwest Journal Press to help you on your journey.

———

BY EARL NIGHTINGALE:

How to Completely Change Your Life in 30 Seconds[1]

Why Ninety-Five Fail, Only Five Succeed[2]

How to Prevent Stress From Ruining Your Life[3]

How to Mine Your Own Acres of Diamonds[4]

How Creative People Win[5]

2 Amazing Ways to Solve Your Problems[6]

7 Strange Secrets to Winning Big[7]

The $25,000 Idea[8]

---

1. https://livesensical.com/book/completely-change-your-life-30-seconds/

2. https://livesensical.com/book/ninety-five-fail-five-succeed-earl-nightingale/

3. https://livesensical.com/book/prevent-stress-ruining-life/

4. https://livesensical.com/book/entrepreneurship-mine-acres-diamonds/

5. https://livesensical.com/book/creative-people-win-earl-nightingale/

6. https://livesensical.com/book/creative-people-win-earl-nightingale/

7. https://livesensical.com/book/
   7-strange-secrets-winning-big-get-happy-money-health/

8. https://livesensical.com/book/25000-idea-simple-ways-effective-goal-achievement/

Earl Nightingale's Strangest Secret Library[9]

BY NAPOLEON HILL:

The Updated and Complete Think and Grow Rich[10]

The Master Key to Riches[11]

The Magic Ladder to Success[12]

10 Easy Lessons in Cosmic Habitforce[13]

The Law of Success[14]

BY J. B. JONES:

If You Can Count to Four...[15]

How to Get Everything You Want Out of Life[16]

BY CLAUDE M. BRISTOL:

Magic of Believing – the Science of Goal Achievement[17]

9. https://livesensical.com/book/earl-nightingales-strangest-secret-library/

10. https://livesensical.com/book/think-grow-rich-updated-complete/

11. https://livesensical.com/book/master-key-riches-sequel-think-grow-rich/

12. https://livesensical.com/book/magic-ladder-success-prequel-think-grow-rich/

13. https://livesensical.com/book/10-easy-lessons-cosmic-habitforce/

14. https://livesensical.com/book/law-success-law-attraction/

15. https://livesensical.com/book/
    if-you-can-count-to-four-by-james-breckenridge-jones-self-improvement-books/

16. https://livesensical.com/book/get-everything-want-life/

The Magic of Believing Collection[18]

BY DOROTHEA BRANDE:

Wake Up and Live![19]

BY WALLACE D. WATTLES:

Science of Getting Rich[20]

BY DR. ROBERT C. WORSTELL:

Freedom Is - period[21]

Winning Your Infinite Freedom[22]

Make Yourself Great Again![23]

The Art of Wonk[24]

OR VISIT OUR ONLINE bookstore at:

---

17. https://livesensical.com/book/magic-believing-science-goal-achievement/

18. https://calm.li/MOB-Coll

19. https://livesensical.com/book/wake-live-dorothea-brande/

20. https://livesensical.com/book/science-getting-rich/

21. https://livesensical.com/book/freedom-period-dr-robert-c-worstell/

22. https://livesensical.com/book/winning-infinite-freedom-complete-series-2006-2011/

23. https://livesensical.com/book/make-great-complete-collection-mindset-stacking/

24. https://livesensical.com/book/art-wonk-compleat/

https://calm.li/LivingSensical

DON'T MISS OUT!

———

Want to keep up to date with this author and all upcoming books?

Find out about special discounts?

Hear about pre-release specials, new audiobooks and courses?!?

Instant Access – Join Here

Click or type into your browser:

http://livesensical.com/go/author-specials/

DID YOU LIKE THIS BOOK?

HOW ABOUT LEAVING A review with the vendor?

Otherwise (or in addition) you can leave your recommendations on:

- **Bookbub**[1]

The whole point is to enable others to find books that you liked reading.

Which then helps you find more great books to read.

And...

Feel free to share this book!

---

1. https://www.bookbub.com/recommendations

Did you love *Freedom Is (Period.) 2.0*? Then you should read *Make Yourself Great Again - Complete Collection*[2] by Dr. Robert C. Worstell!

[3]

You're Already Wired for Exceptional Success

BUT: Those same programs also have given you your greatest failures.

If you've ever had a complete melt-down, a real failure of your mindset, where the world has seemingly gone to hell and stayed there, you're not alone.

it's just sad to tell you that it's your own damned fault.

What makes it worse is to find out that all you need to succeed was already programmed into you – and has been since you were born.

---

2. https://books2read.com/u/mV7kQA

3. https://books2read.com/u/mV7kQA

Then how did you get into that mess?

By believing what people told you- as you were raised,- and in every school you went to,- all your on the job training,- every movie you ever saw,- or song you ever heard.

All those lessons and examples just helped you believe in something other than your own ability to become great.

Most of what we are told these days are that the environment makes the individual. However, this has only really been taught since just after World War II. Long, long before that, there were many schools of thought which held that the individual creates their own success in this world, or lack of it.

And that is a far longer tradition, across our 10,000 years of culture, back through our verbal traditions and storytellers.

Some of our oldest traditions, such as the Tibetan Book of the Dead, say that as children we have complete access to all the world's knowledge – up to the point we learn to talk. And other traditions say that we can each still tap into unlimited knowledge. Some studies begun in the 1950's and verified through testing, have shown this to still be true.

Unfortunately, this isn't what Conventional Wisdom says. Most Science disagrees. And it isn't what any government or school wants you to believe. All the best authorities...

However, one of the oldest phrases, published in books in various formats throughout all of our recorded works, says the same thing in various ways:

We Become What We Think About.

What you think and how you think is up to you. How you think consistently, the mental habits you've developed, are those you chose for yourself.

If you build those mental habits stacked on top of unproved, untested data, then you risk your sanity because you listened to all these sources and chose to think that way.

The economic crash of 2008 affected a lot of people adversely. But a lot more people survived.

The U.S. election of 2016 affected a lot of people adversely. But a lot more people survived.

There will always be more adverse situations ahead. Because that's the cyclical history of this mudball we live on.

But you don't have to repeat these failures, these crashes.

And now, this story is complete.

This series of 4 books now answers all the questions and takes you right back to the beginning to learn even more. Because this subject is as deep as you want to take it. You are referenced to current newsmakers as examples as well as principles back before our 10,000 years of history started.

This is a landmark volume you'll want as a reference, along with its sister handbook, The Strangest Secret Library. And your life is guaranteed to never be the same...

Get Your Copy Now.

Read more at https://livesensical.com/book-author/ dr-robert-c-worstell/.

Also by Dr. Robert C. Worstell

Change Your Life Toolset
Get Your Self Scam Free

Make Yourself Great Again Library
Why You Got All That Stuff
The Art of Wonk, Compleat

Masters of Copywriting
Breakthrough Copywriter 2.0: An Advertising Field Guide to Eugene M. Schwartz' Classic
John E Kennedy - Reason Why Advertising - With Intensive Advertising

Mindset Stacking Guides
Make Yourself Great Again Part 1
Make Yourself Great Again Part 2
Make Yourself Great Again Part 3
Make Yourself Great Again Part 4

Choose. Believe. Win.
Make Yourself Great Again - Complete Collection
Go Thunk Yourself, Again!
The Strangest Secret Collection 2.0
Think Less and Grow Richer
Freedom Is (Period.) 2.0

PMA Science of Success
Napoleon Hill's PMA: Science of Success Course - An Introduction

Really Simple Writing & Publishing
How To Write And Publish For Free
Backwards Book Publishing: Save Time, Earn More, Work Less
Writing-Publishing Survival Guide
Author Freedom Guidebook
How to Stop Feeding the Beast
A Completely Unauthorized Instafreebie Guidebook
How I Survived My First Year of Fiction Writing
How to Become an Instant Author in 30 Seconds
Becoming a Wealthy Writer
Marketers & Writers - Scammers & Dupes
How to Write Less and Profit More - Version 2.0
Writing Serial Fiction In the Real World 2.0

Standalone
Farm Less, Profit More: Lessons in Regenerative Grazing

Watch for more at https://livesensical.com/book-author/
dr-robert-c-worstell/.